Understanding Information

An Introduction

ERNST & YOUNG
CENTER FOR INFORMATION TECHNOLOGY AND STRATEGY

Macmillan Information Systems Series

Series Editor: Professor Ian O. Angell
Department of Information Systems
London School of Economics

Understanding Information

An Introduction

Jonathan Liebenau
James Backhouse

Department of Information Systems
London School of Economics

MACMILLAN

First edition 1990

Published by
MACMILLAN EDUCATION LTD
Houndmills, Basingstoke, Hampshire RG21 2XS
and London
Companies and representatives
throughout the world

Printed in Great Britain by
Billing & Sons Ltd, Worcester

Cartoons by Frank Nichols

British Library Cataloguing in Publication Data
Liebenau, Jonathan
Understanding information : an introduction.
1. Computer systems
I. Title   II. Backhouse, James
004
ISBN 0–333–53680–0

Contents

Preface

This book is intended primarily as a textbook for students of information systems, information technology and computer science. Students of management or administration who will be involved in establishing large information systems may also find it pertinent. It brings together material from a large variety of disciplines, including sociology, semiotics and management, as well as philosophical and anthropological studies of information. For this reason, it may be of interest to students in other areas who are concerned with the integration of these fields.

We have designed this book to be used as a central text for a whole course spanning one semester or term; but because it has many exercises and guidelines for further work, it may also be used more flexibly. Each chapter is preceded by a short outline of the main points so that students can anticipate the range of material covered and the goals inherent in each section. At the end of each chapter are suggested discussion points and exercises. Extra provision is made for chapters 3-6 so that the book can easily be used in the American 14-week semester as well as the British 10-week term. Finally, there is a short selection of "Suggested reading," with indications of how other works relate to points in the chapter.

The **Introduction** shows how various definitions have been used by people in different disciplines and with different ideas about what constitutes information. We consider the various approaches to studying it and show why, although the topic is intrinsically interdisciplinary, it is crucial to understand information when analyzing, designing, establishing, and managing information systems. Unfortunately, where people have concentrated on computer based systems or allowed the requirements of data processing to become central to organizational structure, they have usually lost sight of what information actually does to and for an organization. This chapter shows how to avoid this fundamental misconception.

Part I, on **Semiotics and Information**, sets out the basis for understanding information. In the chapter on **Semiotics** we show a conceptual breakdown of the levels of information systems into four parts. This helps us to identify the range of issues from the cultural environment and problems of meaning to formal structures and the physical characteristics of codes and signals. The first level, **Pragmatics**, is concerned with the actual context of activity and those characteristics of people, organizations and acts of communication which affect information. Here we examine how people use shared assumptions and "common knowledge," how ambiguities arise and how they are dealt with, and how the essentially informal nature of human interaction controls the largest part of what we call information. The second level, **Semantics**, brings together the traditional study of problems of meaning in philosophy and linguistics with our special concern about how information takes on meaning. Here we introduce the tools of semantic analysis and build models of networks of meaning which might later be formalized so as to become a component of the bridge between informal and formal systems. Moving further towards formality, the section on **Syntactics** starts with a review of natural and formal languages as studied by linguists and shows how the logical construction of elements of syntax can help us to identify the utility and limitations of formalisms. Finally, we consider the place of communication theory and the theory of information as expressed by mathematicians and systems engineers in the section called **Empirics**.

Part II, on **Information and Organizations**, brings together the more theoretical material of semiotics with tangible material on organizations and institutions. First we look at **Computer Systems and Information Systems** and study the organizational contexts in which we typically find problems arising from a too narrow conception of how information functions. Using this as a base we move on to investigate the characteristics of **Formal Systems**, and especially the place of rule based systems. Here we consider the differences between rule based systems which are machine driven, or incorporated into the software of a computer based system, and those systems which are manual, or guided by rules which are written down and learned by practitioners. We go on to examine the problem of using computer based systems in informal contexts for which they are not suited. We also consider where rule based systems might benefit from being implemented in computer software. This is followed by a section which brings together the conceptual material on social systems with the empirical material on computer based and other formal systems, and concentrates on **Informal Systems**. Here we show how formal systems must fit into informal systems, and we provide guidelines on how to go about systematically studying the informal aspects of information.

We conclude with an analysis of how the various threads of issues studied can be brought together to give us a coherent view of both the underlying principles and the applications of the study of information systems. Following the theme set out at the beginning of the book, we can see that social organizations are primary to the conceptualization of the use and meaning of information, and therefore to everything we need to know about it. That social organization must be studied in conjunction with all other aspects of information is at the base of our approach.

Who studies information as an academic discipline? There are a number of longstanding academic departments which have recently begun to organize their teaching and research around the concept of information, information systems, or information management. These include computer science departments at one extreme and management studies departments at the other. In between there are a number of groups whose titles, revealing their origins, might include terms such as systems analysis, management of information systems (or "MIS" in business schools), management sciences, decision analysis, or operations research. Some groups, well entrenched in other disciplines such as software engineering and "information science," also include some study of information and the structure of information systems.

Information also plays an important role in other disciplines, and in recent years people in departments as far apart as political science and civil engineering have begun to pay attention to how information is used in organizations.

This is, nevertheless, a young discipline and one strongly dependent upon the work of people whose intention was to contribute elsewhere. In our effort to provide a synthetic introduction, we have diminished the differences in approach that readers of the primary literature face. These approaches are apparent, however, in the books proposed as "Suggested reading." The first step avid students might take would be to explore this rich diversity on their own, with this text as a guide.

Acknowledgements

This text is a product of ideas developed in a course taught at the London School of Economics since 1973 as part of a master's degree program for systems analysis. Taught for many years by Ronald Stamper, the course provided an introduction to the study of information and was based on his book, *Information in Business and Administrative Systems* (Wiley, 1974). That book showed how to conceive of the integration of the myriad of issues which underlie the use of information in organizations and we are indebted to Ronald for both ideas and support. In the intervening years there has not only been tremendous change in information technology, but also a confluence of ideas from various sources about the character of information *per se*. This text provides a new foundation for students who will need to manage information and the new information technology. It is an accessible text, an interpretative text, and a major revision of previous ideas about where stresses should lie and how best to teach information management.

Professor Ian Angell of the London School of Economics suggested to us that we write this book. Our students, both at the master's degree level who studied in the lecture course in which the chapters of this text were presented in the academic years 1988-89 and 1989-90, and numerous doctoral students of the department of information systems were of great help.

We thank the BAA plc for permission to use the extract from their advertisement, "Watch your body language," included on page 28.

1 Introduction

- *Definitions*
- *The study of information*
- *Analysis and design*

Have we really entered into an information society? Is our nation a part of the information economy? Have our offices become plugged into an elaborate information system? What is information, anyway? In this chapter we look at how different people interpret the concept of information, and then consider what is inadequate about those interpretations and work towards an understanding of information which will allow us to see more clearly how organizations make use of it.

"Information" is in some ways an unfortunate term because it has come to mean a myriad of things. The way the word is used is perhaps a good indicator of the prejudices and intentions of the user, but it is often used in a careless or imprecise manner. In most day-to-day situations this is not a serious difficulty, but for any careful study of information and information systems it is important that users are at least aware of the variety of definitions and ascriptions given to it. These range in meaning from definitions so narrow and uninformative as to obscure the difference between data and information to those so broad and unspecific as to fail to distinguish information from anything else which might be communicated; for some governments "information" has come to replace the discredited term, "propaganda."

Definitions

Numerous definitions have been proposed for the term "information," and most of them serve well the narrow interests of those defining it. Consider the following concepts, drawn from a wide range of sources.

Information is knowledge communicated concerning some particular fact, subject, or event.[1]

1) The communication or reception of knowledge or intelligence.
2) Knowledge obtained from investigation, study, or instruction.[2]

The terms "information" and "data" are sometimes used synonymously with "information," supplanting "data" in contexts where the emphasis is on the broad, grand or useful aspects: "information processing," "information network," "information interchange."[3]

Information is only a measure of the difficulty in transmitting the sequences [i.e. messages] produced from some information source.[4]

Data are language, mathematical, or other symbolic surrogates which are generally agreed upon to represent people, objects, events and concepts. . . . Information is the result of modelling, formatting, organizing or converting data in a way that increases the level of knowledge for its recipient.[5]

The distillation of data through its being processed results in the creation of information.[6]

The meaning of information is precisely the reduction in uncertainty.[7]

Information is a pattern or design that rearranges data for instrumental purposes.[8]

Information is data recorded, classified, organized, related or interpreted within context to convey meaning.[9]

Information is the reduction of uncertainty. In information theory, one "bit" of information is the amount required to allow one to choose between two alternatives.[10]

These definitions are all problematic. They contradict one another and therefore we are left to choose either the best definition or the best combination of definitions for our purposes. Some definitions regard information as something which is measurable. Others link it to something which is done to data. Still others regard it as something which can be patterned, or something related to uncertainty. There is no consensus.

However, because it is a word in such common use, we are bound to face difficulty in communicating our particular use of the term to others when that need arises. Most importantly, these definitions fail to provide an adequate basis for understanding information.

For our purposes it is important to identify at least the following elements: information cannot exist independently of the receiving person who gives it meaning and somehow acts upon it. That action usually includes analysis or at least interpretation, and the differences between data and information must be preserved, at least in so far as information is data arranged in a meaningful way for some perceived purpose.

The study of information

The study of information provides opportunities for bringing together a number of component disciplines. It offers the basis for studying organizations, widespread communication problems, and the role of computing and mechanical manipulation from a common perspective. The scale of problems encountered in large organizations, or even small businesses which invest a significant amount of their time and resources into information systems, has focused attention on the issue.

For the academic community as well as for professionals in government and industry, the International Federation of Information Processing [IFIP] is a central organizing body and its areas of concentration are revealing. The main streams of concern include:
* Formal aspects of organizational systems and methods of information requirements analysis
* Impacts upon organizations of computer based systems
* Decision support systems
* Office automation
* Database management systems
* Social impacts of computing and telecommunications
* Privacy and data security.

People working on information problems tackle them from many different approaches. These approaches are derived from the treatment of information in various academic disciplines ranging from electrical engineering to business administration. When engineers face an information problem they may first look at the signalling or coding of messages. When computer professionals encounter the same problem, they may look first at the logic of the data structures. Consider the perspective of office managers. They will be concerned with office interactions and look first at how to interpret guidelines and procedures. We might expect top executives of large organizations to have an entirely different perspective and be more concerned with looking at the broad context of the enterprise. They may focus on long term trends, the business culture, and the image that the business has in the eyes of its customers. Let us consider each of these four different approaches in turn.

Engineers would apply an understanding of the problem of communicating information in terms of the signalling and coding of messages and would use tools of analysis which go deep into the physical aspects of the process. Electronic means of communication are suitable for such analysis because the training of modern engineers gives them an appropriate conceptual approach. Their concept of information generally starts from a model which interprets the communication process as one of generating signals, coding them, transmitting them, and then decoding them. The tools at their disposal include an array of engineering theories, procedures of technical analysis, and the means to intervene in all the various mechanisms.

Computer professionals might view the problem from the standpoint of systems analysis and programming. The starting point might be an analysis of the use of data in terms of data structures and data flows. Problems which lend themselves to these skills would be those of logic and syntax. Their model might be one based on the input, storage, processing and output of data. They would apply tools based on software design techniques such as models of the data used in organizations and the data flows that support them.

Managers are expected to give an organization structures and procedures which allow it effectively to perform functions associated with its purposes. For them, information carries meanings which can be interpreted in terms of intended actions, prescriptions, or guidelines. Managers are concerned with the means of controlling operations. To exercise that control they apply managerial techniques which might include restructuring an organization, changing an incentive scheme, or deploying the means for staff to understand messages more easily.

People at the top of large organizations are expected to view information differently. They would be concerned with the context of a business, perhaps its public image, the business culture which permeates the staff, and the long term trends of that organization and those which affect it. Their view of information is something which is used to understand specific and general aspects of these issues. They may work to change organizations by, for example, moving them from one location to another, adjusting their financial base, or cultivating an image through major changes in advertising or public relations.

All of these four views are relevant to different elements of communication in organizations. Our challenge is to hold together these apparently disparate approaches in such a way as to be able to use information to control, to construct, to improve, in short, to manage organizations. An understanding of the broadest interpretation of the concept of information can show why information is in the social domain and can best be handled as a managerial or administrative issue. This takes the analysis of information beyond the arena of the technician and brings it into the realm of people from all different parts of an enterprise.

Analysis and design

By taking advantage of the opportunities made available by this synthetic approach we can work on highly complex organizational problems. This approach allows us to break them down into discrete elements and tackle each element in an appropriate way. This then allows us to concentrate on one particular aspect at a time, to undertake our analysis and design of the problem, while retaining the relationship between the part and the whole.

As a result of the rapid growth in business organizations and the increased opportunities which that growth allows, we now face increasing demand for information about finance, markets, staff, and all the other things which make large organizations work. Better quality information has enabled managers to exercise control over highly complex structures. That very complexity fuels the need for ever more information for sophisticated decision making. The quantity of information commonly generated in large organizations has exceeded the capacity of traditional analytical approaches. A proper understanding of information can help us to examine complex questions about information.

For example, consider a pizzeria where the proprietor wants to decide on new ways for customers to order a pizza. The management may be willing to retain the old system where customers will have to place their orders in person, but it may be evaluating other methods, such as telephone orders or a fax machine. The decision could be taken on a variety of levels. The manager can look at it as a technical issue, such as might concern the installation of a new telephone switchboard. Alternatively, the problem might be seen as a logical one about how orders are processed and stored. Another way of looking at the same problem would be from the point of view of increasing sales by whatever means of ordering speeds up the process of selling pizzas. Or, a fax ordering service might be the most fashionable thing to offer at the time, something which changes the image of the restaurant from an ordinary corner pizzeria into a trendy new business. It matters very much how the problem is viewed.

Throughout this book we will be coming back to the Echo pizzeria to look at how different aspects of information affect the business. Imagine a friendly, family business of modest scale, of about fourteen employees working two shifts per day, seven days a week. As is typical of such restaurants, they have a big take-out business as well as a small dining room. We will be introducing other elements as we go along and take into account some of the normal things which we might expect the business to encounter, such as staff problems and opportunities for growth. Each time the example is used it is linked explicitly to some broad issues and it is implicitly associated with the general situation of business, large as well as small.

In a small scale, relatively informal context, the participants have a feeling for how to use information, how much information is appropriate, who needs it, and how to transmit it. In a household kitchen, there is no need to worry about how the cook uses information in relation to the family. But for our pizzeria, or any other formal organization, rules are needed to direct and control the use of information. This is especially so when computer systems are involved, and is all the more extreme in the case of, for example, telecommunications networks.

In formal organizations someone must always decide what information is needed by whom, when, where, and how. Although these problems are resolved informally in the family kitchen, in a formal organization managerial decision makers deal with them and they usually do not have the resources and analytical skills to do so effectively. Typically, they have looked to information technology to solve such problems. This has led to a massive increase in the amount of information available at any time; an amount which is perhaps disproportionate to the capacity to make use of it.

Analysis and design is what people do when they set up information systems in organizations. Typically, they approach the task with the computer in mind and look for characteristics of organizations or ways of restructuring them for computer based systems. We approach analysis and design initially as a set of tasks separate from that of constructing computer systems. Later we will consider how computers fit in.

In summary, our approach concentrates on the following themes:

1. Using information is a process of manipulating signs.
2. Information is integral to organizations.
3. Using information is a social process.

In the chapters that follow we show how the complexity of large scale information systems can be understood by approaching the notion of information from the semiotic perspective. The strength of this perspective is that it incorporates the disparate points of view of top executives, managers, computer professionals and engineers.

Discussion issues

1. Consider the range of common uses for the term "information." Which ones can be reconciled with the use of the term in this book? Why is it difficult to reconcile others?

2. Apply the approaches of an engineer, computer professional, manager and top executive to information problems in an organization that you know. Discuss how different skills must be used for different parts of the same problem.

3. How can analysis be used by managers to provide better quality information?

Exercises

1. Consider the following sources of data. Can they become sources of information? If so, explain how.
   a) an on-line stock market telex in a hotel lobby.
   b) a list of daily temperatures from around the world in a newspaper.
   c) the flashing of a lighthouse beacon in the harbor.

2. A new internal telephone system is being installed in your office. Analyze why it will be viewed distinctly by an electrical engineer, a computer programmer, an office manager, and a chief executive.

3. From other textbooks that you are using, collect examples of various applications of the concept of information. Develop a classification scheme for these examples, such as information as signals, as data, as a process, and other categories which seem appropriate.

Suggested reading

Kent, W., *Data and Reality*, New York: North Holland, 1978.
This essay looks at the difficulty of reflecting the organization in abstract data models. Kent sees the flaws in the common models of data and information.

Panko, R., *End User Computing*, New York: Wiley, 1988.
> This is an up-to-date textbook for beginning computer users. It is especially strong on introducing concepts for the design of business information systems. By focusing on the end user, Panko avoids a narrow technical perspective.

Stamper, Ronald, *Information in Business and Administrative Systems*, New York: Wiley, 1974.
> A general and complete introduction to this subject which provides coverage of the material at an advanced level. Although it is out-of-date in part, Stamper's is an approach sympathetic to that of this textbook.

Notes:

1. *Oxford English Dictionary.*
2. *Webster's Collegiate Dictionary.*
3. G. Frank (ed), *Dictionary of Computing*, New York: Wiley 1982.
4. C.E. Shannon and Weaver, W., *The Mathematical Theory of Communication*, Urbana: University of Illinois Press, 1949.
5. J. Burch, et al., *Information Systems: Theory and Practice*, Santa Barbara, Calif.: Hamilton, 1974.
6. H.D. Clifton, *Business Data Systems*, Englewood Cliffs, N.J.: Prentice-Hall, 1978.
7. K.J. Arrow, *The Economics of Information*, Cambridge, Mass.: Belnap, 1984.
8. D. Bell, "The Social Framework of the Information Society," in M.L. Detouzos and J. Moses, *The Computer Age, A twenty year view*, Cambridge, Mass.: MIT, 1979.
9. S.C. Blumenthal, *Management Information Systems*, Englewood Cliffs, N.J.: Prentice Hall, 1969.
10. A. Whyte, "The environment and social behaviour," in H. Tajfel & C. Fraser, *Introducing Social Psychology*, Harmondsworth: Penguin, 1978.

Part I

Semiotics and Information

In the following five chapters we will build the foundation for applied studies of information systems. This foundation will necessarily be somewhat theoretical, although we will also work through a number of concrete examples as we proceed and apply the concepts tangibly. The process is cumulative and built in a gradual manner. After the chapter which introduces the semiotic approach to looking at the general character of information, the following four chapters can roughly be divided in half. The first two consider the issues most closely related to social contexts, uses and meanings. The next two deal with the areas of most concern to engineers and computer professionals and demonstrate how they are interlinked.

Each chapter combines an analytical element with a broad discussion of the general issues involved. Taken together they provide different kinds of tools which form the basis for further analysis of organizations, as described in Part II.

2 Introduction to semiotics

- *What is communication?*
- *Signs*
- *Signs and machines*

Communication consists of elements which we can analyze in terms of a continuum from context through meaning, grammar and code. An act of communication has been successful when the intentions of the sender are understood by the receiver.

What is communication?

Communication is a process which involves at least two parties. This process can be characterized as a set of activities involving a sender with intentions to convey, a medium or channel for carrying signals, and a receiver who has the ability to interpret those signals. In a typical telephone conversation there is a sender who has something to say, a telecommunications network which is the medium or channel, and the person at the other end of the line who is the receiver. The intention to convey is in the mind of the sender and forms the reason for making the telephone call. The sender will ascertain that a connection is made by listening for someone to pick up the telephone and say "hello." Then they will need to establish that they are speaking to the right person by listening for a familiar voice or asking for someone in particular by name or description.

Given the way that we have defined communication, anchored to the intentions of the agents and their ability to interpret, this is best seen as a social phenomenon. The pattern is governed by social expectations and procedures, and the technical elements, for example of a telephone system, serve only as one means of facilitating interaction among people. Communication usually takes place without any special technical facility, because it is usually face-to-face. In mass communication, elaborate technical facilities are required, and this is presupposed when we speak of computer based systems. The technical characteristics, however, concern the signalling elements in this process and nothing else. The machinery has no bearing on the intentions, the meaning, or the interpretation of signals.

Effective communication takes place when there is a high degree of correspondence between the sender's intentions and the receiver's interpretation. The ultimate test for success is when there is an appropriate response, but for this some sort of feedback is necessary. That was a requirement, for example, when pilots were sent messages and had to respond with a phrase such as "Roger, and out." In a business, a marketing manager might know that his intentions have been effectively communicated when the market responds favorably with increased sales.

"ROGER AND OUT!"

Because of the complex of different elements involved in communication, messages often fail to perform the functions for which they were intended. Communication has broken down when, for example, we try to order a pizza by telephone from the pizzeria and it fails to be delivered. We might have thought that we had made a good connection and expressed our order clearly and believed that the person at the other end took down our order. But the pizza has not arrived. The cause of a breakdown might be in any of the areas associated with the intentions, the medium, the signal or the receiver and their ability to interpret.

Detecting a fault might require a systematic investigation of the entire communication process and all of the elements involved. It is for this reason that we need analytical tools which can address the problem comprehensively.

Signs

Communication takes place by the use of signs which have a number of properties. Let us consider these properties of signs in terms of four levels within which we can apply different analytical tools. These levels represent a range from the most social to the most technical aspects of communication.

The levels can be see in two parts. **Pragmatics** and **semantics** roughly correspond to the content and purpose of communication. **Syntactics** and **empirics** roughly correspond to the form and means. The entire structure presupposes that responsible agents, which might be individuals, groups, or larger organizations, have commitments, expectations and relations within social frameworks. These reflect the ability of actors with thoughts to have an effect upon the world.

The first, which takes into account the general culture and broad context of communication, is referred to as pragmatics. In pragmatics we take account of the assumptions, expectations and beliefs of the agents involved, and we assess them in relation to the social environment in which signs are being used. For example, when we order a pizza by telephone, we do so expecting that the receiver of the call shares the same assumptions we do. So, when we ask for it to be delivered, we assume that pizzerias transport orders to addresses on request.

The second level is that which concerns meaning and knowledge and is called semantics. In the semantic level we take account of the connections that agents make between the signs that they use and their behavior and actions. So, having established that the pizzeria delivers, analysis at the semantic level allows us to concentrate on the precise meaning of the term "delivery," and will determine what is meant by the concept that the pizza will arrive in a reasonable time and in good shape.

The third level is that of logic and grammar and is called syntactics. Syntactics provides us with the tools for the construction of formal rules and the means by which they interrelate. Syntax is a part of any act of communication and governs the way that we use language, but it also concerns the rules associated with the implicit contract that we enter into when we telephone to order a pizza. Having established that the pizzeria delivers and that we understand what a delivery is, syntactics provides the rules within which the order for a delivery is made. For example, a pizza order must consist of at least the type of pizza, its size, and a full address and telephone number.

The final level is the one which describes the codes, signals and physical characteristics of the medium of communication and is called empirics. Empirics includes the activities usually associated with communications engineers such as the statistical description of the speed and quantity of signals, or the mechanisms for encoding and decoding. Having established the first three layers, empirics provides the analytical framework within which we can understand the physics and electronics of the telephone system that we use to order our pizza.

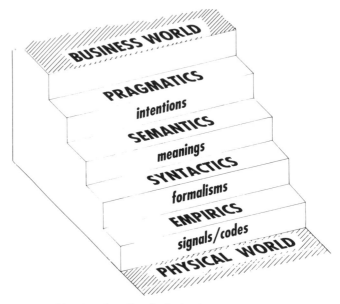

The steps from the physical to the business world

Most information systems are difficult to understand when you first look at them and require an analytical approach. The approach described above, derived from the characteristics of signs, allows the analyst to see how information systems operate as sign processing systems where people do the processing. It allows us to identify problems which would not otherwise have come to our attention. Then we can examine the different properties of signs employed in the system, and the understanding which comes from that examination contributes to our ability to design better information systems.

The process of analyzing signs and how they function is called **semiotics**. The levels introduced above represent the four main branches of semiotics. Anything can be a sign so long as it can be perceived and interpreted: gestures, words, numbers, ceremonies. Consider the signs which might be used in our pizzeria. A customer would raise his arm to attract the attention of the waiter. This gesture is a sign. Language also provides signs used, in this case, to order the pizza. Numbers can be signs for objects and menus commonly number the items available, so "4" might refer to the pepperoni pizza. A full restaurant is a sign for the quality of the food served. The pizza you ate becomes a sign for the pizzas you might or might not eat in the future. Using one object as a sign for another object is a different sort of sign; for example, waiters speak of "table" to stand for a group of customers, as in the phrase "Have you served table 9 yet?" Ceremonies are very complex signs, but we can easily see that the pizzeria opening party is a public sign that marks the beginning of business. Anything can be a sign.

Signs can be classified into groups: an **index** relates the sign to what it signifies by referring to its intensity. We might speak of the greenness of a field indicating its fertility, or the blackness of the cloud indicating the severity of the coming weather. An **icon** acts upon the senses in much the same way as what they refer to does. In visual terms, an architect's model of a building presents itself to our senses in a way similar to the building on which it is based. **Signs** and **symbols** have the most loose connection to their referent. A red traffic light signifies that the driver should stop, but this connection rests upon a social or legal convention. The successful interpretation of signs results in information.

Semiotics in its modern form came out of linguistics and philosophy of language. The pioneering French linguist, Ferdinand de Saussure applied the concept of the change of relations among signs to problems of historical linguistics in his 1916 text on general linguistics. The study was made more sophisticated by the American philosopher Charles Morris, some of whose work is described in Chapter 4. Applications of semiotic methods were highly influential in anthropology after the imaginative work of Claude Levi-Strauss in the late 1950s. His book on structuralism in anthropology brought semiotics into the structuralist school which proceeded to apply it to a wide range of topics.

Literary criticism has been the area where it is most enthusiastically applied by those who wish to be able to take a story apart like an object of anthropological study. Sometimes this has gone too far and led to a stodgy approach which separates the use of signs too much from their context. Nevertheless, the results of this work have been especially useful for highly symbolic texts, including theological writings, and also for symbolic art forms. It has also been subtly applied to analyze the sign relations in some ordinary texts, and it has been extremely popular as a means of analyzing and creating advertisements. Other recent applications have been in political science, where it has been used as a means of coming to understand complex and changing relations among nations. Finally, no review of the use and impact of semiotics could be complete without a mention of the extraordinary popularizing effect of Umberto Eco's semiotic thriller novel, *The Name of the Rose*.

Signs and machines

Using a semiotic approach allows the analyst to come much closer to understanding the key elements of information systems than do other methods. It addresses directly the meaning and use of information within an organization. Since information technology is concerned with storing symbols which organizations use to achieve their aims, it is highly appropriate that the analytical method centers upon the question of how signs relate to communication.

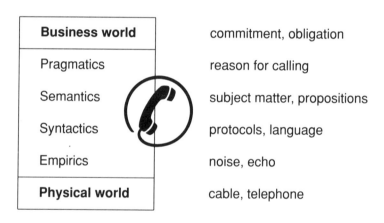

Business world	commitment, obligation
Pragmatics	reason for calling
Semantics	subject matter, propositions
Syntactics	protocols, language
Empirics	noise, echo
Physical world	cable, telephone

Semiotic analysis of telephone call

Semiotic analysis can function as a diagnostic tool. When problems arise, the analyst will not necessarily know at what level the breakdown has occurred. When we consider the broad character of information systems, we can apply the semiotic levels quite easily. Take the failure of an act of communication using a telephone. The telephone call is, to begin with, something which exists in a social setting. It would presuppose social expectations, commitments, obligation. At the pragmatic level, there would be a reason for calling. Here we can see that there is a particular culture and context in which information is used. This is the level at which analysis begins. From there, the focus shifts to problems of the semantics of the subject matter, the content, and the propositions expressed. The language used and the etiquette of telephoning is the concern of the syntactic level. In so far as this communication takes place through electronic equipment, issues such as the bandwidths, noises and distortions of the signal transmission will be the concern of the empirics level. Finally, there are physical attributes of the channel such as the telephone itself and its cables.

With this sort of analysis, the problem solver will not need to waste time on levels which are functioning well. In particular, problems on a syntactic and empiric level are generally more technical in character, whereas problems which arise in the semantic and pragmatic areas are more social in character. Once an analysis has been made, the problem can be identified and dealt with.

The semiotic approach to analyzing information systems is robust and independent of any particular technology. Instead, because it is based upon the way people use signs, it can come close to capturing the full range of properties.

Discussion issues

1. Discuss how advertising can be analyzed along semiotic lines. Consider
    the way the following structure can be applied to specific advertisements.
    social: customer expectations, supplier responsibility
    pragmatic: purpose of advertisement
    semantic: content of advertisement
    syntactic: layout, presentation
    empiric: readership and reader behavior
    physical: media chosen

2. An office network uses information technology in a variety of ways.
    Discuss how a semiotic analysis can be applied to reveal the different
    approaches taken by people in various positions when the office manager
    fails to get an immediate response from an electronic mail message.

3. Look at the social conventions in your classroom. Apply the approach
    used to analyze the ordering of a pizza by telephone to the actions you go
    through when you wish to contribute to a class discussion.

Exercises

1. Patterns of movement in a crowd can be a sign. When a crowded
    sidewalk is seen from above, any disturbance can easily be noticed by the
    anomaly in movement. For example, if a group of people is milling
    around staring at the sky then we can presume that something unusual is
    occurring. Construct a scenario which explains this phenomenon in terms
    of the signs being given, the media of their transmission and how they
    might be interpreted.

2. Classify the following items into the groups of signs: index, icon, symbol:
    a black cloud
    a graduation ceremony
    an engineer's model
    a "No Entry" sign
    sunburned skin
    a snapshot of the family
    the screech of car tires before a crash

3. You apply for admission to a university and are rejected. Diagnose the possible reasons for being rejected using the semiotic levels of analysis.

Suggested reading

Eco, Umberto, *Introduction to the Theory of Semiotics*, Bloomington: University of Indiana Press, 1976.
A key text on semiotics which sets out in great detail the advanced concept of signs and links it to linguistic and literary theory.

Jervis, Robert, *The Logic of Images in International Relations*, Princeton: Princeton University Press, 1970.
An interesting application of the semiotic approach to international affairs. Jervis uses a structure similar to that in this text.

Levi-Strauss, Claude, *Structural Anthropology*, New York: Basic Books, 1962.
The pioneering work of structuralism which sets out the background for an analysis of the relationships among signs as applied to anthropological cases.

Morris, Charles, *Signs and Signification*, Cambridge, Mass., MIT Press, 1964.
A seminal text by the pioneer of semiotics. Easy to read and includes interesting sections on the semiotics of art and of values.

3 Pragmatics

- *Culture*
- *Context*
- *Thought communities; norms*
- *Intentionality*
- *Speech acts*

How can we come to know the underlying meaning, the truth, of some aspect of knowledge or of an act of communication? We might suppose that we come to know a "real world" of some description through discovering the workings of nature. However, the problem is that we can never be certain that the understanding we have is the same as that of the next person. This sort of problem has long plagued philosophers and is still important for us to confront when considering the character of information. The truth, it seems, is inaccessible. We can know what we believe, and especially so if that knowledge is in some way rooted in our familiar culture, but beyond that it is difficult to be confident of the absolute truth that is being communicated to us. But it is more than just a difficulty if we believe that this outside world is inaccessible to us.

Pragmatics is the term we use to describe the consideration of the context of activity, and those characteristics of people, organizations and acts of communication which affect information. Here we consider how people use shared assumptions and "common knowledge," how ambiguities arise and how they are dealt with, and how the essentially informal nature of human interaction controls the largest part of what is analyzed and passed as information. We need to be able to do this in order to understand the context of an information system and as a basis for analyzing and constructing such systems.

Culture

If we believe that knowledge is mediated by the cultural and social context in which it is produced, transmitted and received, then we have to find ways of analyzing the character of that information within its context. To do that we approach the problem first in terms of the relationship between information and culture.

By culture we mean the set of beliefs and assumptions associated with a community. If we take a strong stand on this, we have to come to terms with different cultures adopting different notions of reality. Or we must at least recognize radically different approaches to imparting information. Because this view implies that there is a variety of kinds of "truth" and all interpretations of knowledge are relative to the cultural context in which they are used, it is called the **relativist** position.

Social setting is primary to information. In order to analyze the character, use and impact of communication, it is necessary to understand the context in which it takes place. That context is composed of the culture of those involved, and language exemplifies its most important feature.

Language acquires its meaning only through personal participation. Correct usage is learned not through reflection but through action. Apprentices learn the vocabulary of their trade while at work. At our pizzeria, for example, you would hear the cooks and counter staff shouting orders to each other. Not only might they abbreviate the names of common orders, they might also use a whole vocabulary of slang and special expressions to communicate quickly and precisely what has been ordered. Of course they have the advantage of a constrained circumstance. Even the most outlandish order will still only be some combination of a limited number of available ingredients prepared in one of a small range of ways. As this "language" becomes increasingly complex, it serves its purposes better and is soon indispensable to cooks. At this stage it is a part of the training necessary for new cooks learning the job. One can construct new behavior by using the language and the context of use constrains it sufficiently so that the meaning is clear. Language is both made by and creates our understanding of context.

Context

When we look at the example of our pizzeria, we see the importance of a context providing meaning when people communicate. We can also see how the content of the message is constrained by its context of use. So when the cook receives an order for something he has never put together before, he is able to understand this new order without ambiguity.

Pragmatics allows us to build a foundation on which to construct further analyses of acts of communication. Only after we have some understanding of the context of use can we begin to analyze the meanings, the forms, and the physical character, of information. Now we can see the utility of pragmatic considerations of the role that language plays in the construction of an information system. Context can also be seen in terms of patterns of behavior which delimit our knowledge, beliefs, and values. Patterns of behavior must be shared by members of a society so that they can understand one another and that activities can be coordinated. Organizational failure can often be explained by a breakdown in communication.

In our pizzeria, imagine what would happen if the regular cook calls in sick and a substitute with experience at another pizzeria takes his place. She might know very well how to cook pizzas, but she does not know the terms employed in our pizzeria. Until she learns them there is going to be difficulty in communicating the intentions of our customers. Her assumptions about what a request means would not necessarily be the same as the regular cook. Without that background there is much room for misunderstanding. Instead of catering to our eccentric customer who likes bananas on well done pizzas, she interprets the local slang "B" as baloney, and she really burns the pizza when the order indicates "burned" when "crisp" was intended.

We can break down social context into categories such as those used by the sociologist E.T. Hall. He worked with ten general "streams of cultural messages": association, subsistence, gender, territoriality, temporality, learning, recreation and humor, defence, exploitation, and interaction. To see the use of this classification, let us take three of these streams and consider them in more detail.

E.T. Hall's Ten Streams of Cultural Messages

Association
Subsistence
Gender
Territoriality
Temporality
Learning
Recreation and Humor
Defense
Exploitation
Interaction

By temporality we refer to the conventions in an organization which govern the way that time is constructed and used. This includes concepts of duration, lateness and promptness, as well as the normal labels of the passage of time such as "working day," "lunch hour," or "coffee break." When calculating the wages of employees, the use of terms such as "overtime" or "time and a half" are crucial. Organizations have regulations that govern the starts and finishes of all important activities which take place. For example, the processing of an order may be deemed to start from the time when the customer's request is received and to finish when the goods are dispatched and the bill is paid.

Similarly, behavioral conventions are guided by gender. This is the case in all societies, despite the laudable efforts by some to alter all significant discrimination against women, at least in work. The ways in which the sexes are distinguished and the relationships which are permitted between them are fundamental to society. The change which took place with the use of typewriters is exemplary. When the machines were first introduced into offices and the recording of information was an important element of business practice, typing was a man's job. As companies were restructured to use that information, the analysis of typed material became the man's job, while typing itself was relegated to women. A similar process took place when computers were first introduced into offices. Usually men were operators in the early years. Only as word processing and data entry became routine were these positions filled by women while the "masculine" job was the "Director of IT."

Where and when people interact influences the character of their communication. Rapid, informal exchange might be encouraged by common lunch rooms, sports facilities, or well placed coffee machines so that when the boss says "How nice it is to see you bright and early!" you get the message. The same kind of objectives can be approached by formal means. A memorandum about getting to work on time may be as effective if it is clear that ignoring it could lead to a cut in pay. Organizations differ in their ability to create conditions whereby effective interaction can take place, and in the range of choices.

Let us look at the application of this sort of pragmatic analysis as applied to assessing an electronic mail system. By taking a whole analysis we can look at how extensive the impact is and go into some depth in considering a few examples. An electronic mail system uses a computer based network to send messages between distant users. It can be seen as an extension of a manual or postal communication system, and it is often implemented with the intention of replacing or supplementing parts of an existing system.

When an electronic mail system is established in an existing office, the office workers commonly experience problems in adjusting to it. The various kinds of problems can be easily identified if we apply a classification of the local culture such as that offered by Hall. Here we can see, for example, that the relationship people have to the space around them would be immediately affected by such a change. Office workers might be able to work at home more easily if connected through electronic mail. Close collaboration between distant colleagues might be made easy when people normally working on two different floors of a building can feel they are working in tandem without leaving their respective rooms. Similar analyses are possible throughout Hall's classification, but we will look in detail at temporality and interaction.

The pace of an office is punctuated by set periods in the day for activities such as coffee breaks and lunch. These interruptions in the work process are often used for informal discussions about work, joking, and other activities which help to bring groups together. What then, might we expect after an electronic mail system has been introduced? There might be an increase in informal activity as electronic "chit-chat" is added to the other forms of exchange. What took place before only in the lunch breaks now could happen throughout the day. Another effect might concern the expectation that a manual dispatch system is liable to delays. If "delayed in the mail" was a common excuse, with an electronic mail system this response could not be sustained.   Progress reports and work plans which need to meet deadlines could be more timely than before.   The delivery lead time in an electronic mail network might be something like two hours instead of perhaps one day in a manual system.

Office workers interact in a variety of ways, from the most formal committee meetings and working lunches, to consultation by telephone and informal chats in the corridor.   In addition, standard office communication is effected through letters, memos and circulation lists.   Some letters might require the signature of the addressee to confirm receipt.   The implementation of an electronic mail system could affect these forms of interaction in all kinds of ways.   One study showed that face to face encounters between colleagues at distant locations diminished in relation to the increased use of electronic mail, while for those working physically close together there was little change. Project leaders found the electronic mail system convenient for calling *ad hoc* meetings because it was easy to get word around to all team members quickly.

Thought communities; norms

People who share a common culture see the world in a similar way.   Their common experiences have shaped their views, their expectations and their assumptions.   This can be seen easily in communities which are traditionally religious.   The major religions of the world all specify in great detail not only what actions are expected, but they also guide us in our thinking.   But religion is perhaps an easy example.   Let us consider the less overt constraints and guidelines of secular organizations.

In the sub-culture of our pizzeria, the substitute cook has a lot more to learn besides the terminology.   She will be expected to conform to a wide range of informal and formal norms of behavior.   She will be expected to address the other cooks by their first names and she will be expected to learn the names of the regular customers.   Other informal norms might include a regular Thursday night get-together, a particular custom about collecting money for special occasions, or covering up for Fred when he comes in late after a bad night.   There will also be formal norms or rules which the new cook will have to learn.   These might include rules of cleanliness, punctuality and dress.

The sum total of all these informal and formal norms of behavior comprises the common experience shared by all the people who work together in this pizzeria.   Almost as a religion creates a common basis of expectations and assumptions, beliefs and attitudes, so may these shared experiences to a lesser degree.   We can refer to the people who share these experiences as the thought community associated with our little society around this restaurant.

When we are able to identify specific thought communities, we can see the shared assumptions upon which communication will be interpreted. Communication within the thought community is less problematic because the common experience assures that there are fewer ambiguities which lead to misunderstanding and hence a breakdown.

Such may be the cohesion of these thought communities that the significance of what is being communicated is clear even when the methods used are faulty. Imagine that one of the best customers wishes to order his regular mushroom and anchovy pizza but gets flustered and calls it simply an anchovy pizza. Since the staff know full well what he wants, they give him his regular order anyway.

A major characteristic of a thought community is the **norms** which give it shape. These norms are the mechanisms which transmit conventions within the thought community. They can be categorized in the following ways:

> Perceptual - the way we see the world; recognizing patterns
> Cognitive - standardized beliefs and "common" knowledge
> Evaluative - agreement about how objectives can be reached
> Behavioral - predictability of human actions; including etiquette
> Denotative - choices of signs and what they signify

Perceptual norms guide the way a community recognizes patterns with the senses. The particular definition of color, shape and form differ according to the norms of the community so that what might be regarded as an appropriate shade of orange for a warning light for one might appear too yellow to satisfy another community. For example, there are norms which influence us to speak of a blue sea when the color we commonly see might just as well be called grey or green. As for time, there are often very local standards which affect our perception of what a quick process might be, or whether five minutes is an allowable delay. When an interactive computer program takes five minutes to respond, we know something is wrong, but the same time delay before the beginning of a course lecture is commonly within the range of the allowable.

What is accepted as "common" knowledge differs radically from group to group. The best sportsman for Canadians might be a hockey player, while others might find a football player to be the biggest star when evaluative norms are considered. These influence how we feel about things, such as the values we hold, our sense of good and bad, and what we regard as suitably efficient or effective. When people react to change they invoke their sense of an absolute positive or negative, based on their accepted norms. People may, for example, couch their resistance to computerization in such terms.

What constitutes accepted behavior in a given situation will differ from one community to another. This is easily seen when comparing greetings, where what is acceptable ranges from handshakes to kissing cheeks or bowing.

Denotative norms affect our choices of signs and what they stand for. They provide us with the vocabulary which guides us in how signs refer to behavior or to one another.

Norms can be found in every aspect of social interaction, can be manifested formally or informally, and are usually hidden behind the judgements we make, the assumptions we have, the beliefs we hold, and even the notions of reality we tolerate.

Intentionality

In order to understand the analysis of the character of thought in relation to the problems of setting up information systems, we can use the work of the linguistic philosopher John Searle. He provides the basis for an analysis of the structure of human action through the concept of intentionality. The basic form of the problem is one of the classical paradoxes of philosophy: what is the connection between human thoughts and bodies? The problem has plagued philosophers because they assume that the mind is inherently different from physiological functions. If that is the case, then how can we understand the relationships between thought and action? For those of us interested in problems of information the issue is even more crucial because of the need to use signs to communicate intention and the numerous signs and interpreters available.

Often identical signs have different interpreters. Consider the variety of gestures in common use which mean different things in different contexts. Imagine sending a message to a friend that you are going to arrive for dinner: you can write it out on a sheet of paper, you can type it, you can send it by messenger or by telegram. What each of these methods has in common is the same intention. The key to understanding the particular action is the intention that lies behind it.

This concept is well developed for the purposes of the legal system. Imagine that the software company you work for receives an order for the latest version of a popular software package. You send them an older version and they complain and go to court. Before the court reaches its verdict, the intention behind your action will have to be made clear: Did you intend to cheat your customer by getting rid of old stock? Were you careless in packing the order? Or was it a genuine mistake? There are many things happening in the course of an action, but actions do not explain intentionality, because in action what you are doing depends in large part on what you think you are doing. What you are doing is the intention, but how you do it forms the action itself.

Suppose you know that you were negligent. The jury might decide that you are innocent but you would have no problem explaining the difference between innocence and negligence to yourself. You, as the knower and actor, have special access to your intentions.

| In America this means 'A-OK.' | In France it means 'zero.' | In Japan it means 'money.' | In Tunisia it means 'I'll kill you.' |

The problem with analyzing people's actions is that we must dispense with the notion that there is necessarily a direct relationship between types of actions or behaviors and types of bodily movements. We can see this problem in the case of a set of bodily movements which might constitute part of a dance, signalling, an exercise, testing one's muscles, or none of these.

Intentionality, then, is the key notion in understanding the structure of behavior. Mental states have intentionality insofar as they are about something. We believe that something is the case, or desire that something be so, or wish for something to happen. Searle cautions us against getting intentionality confused with the common notion of "intending," which is only one kind of intentionality, along with believing, desiring, hoping, fearing, and other such states.

Searle goes on to distinguish between the content and the type of a state of mind. So that the same content, as with the differences among wanting to leave the room, believing that I will leave the room, and intending to leave the room could still imply different types. These are three different psychological modes or types, but the same content. The content and the type of the state of mind will serve to relate the mental state to the world. That, after all, is why we have minds with mental states: to represent the world to ourselves; to represent how it is, how we would like it to be, how we fear it may turn out, what we intend to do about it and so on. Another feature about such states is that sometimes they cause things to happen. This is somewhat strange, as it means that the cause both represents and brings about the effect, but it is easy enough to understand implicitly.

Examples of intentional states

belief	irritation	guilt
fear	puzzlement	depression
hope	acceptance	contempt
desire	abhorrence	respect
love	aspiration	indignation
hate	amusement	intention
aversion	disappointment	wishing
liking	elation	wanting
disliking	anger	imagining
doubting	admiration	forgiveness
wondering	pleasure	hostility
terror	anxiety	fantasy
joy	pride	shame
affection	remorse	lust
expectation	sorrow	disgust
rejoicing	grief	animosity

In sum, there are three features of intentionality of central importance. First, intentional states contain ideas of a certain mental type. Second, they determine their conditions of satisfaction, that is, they will be satisfied or not depending on whether the world matches the content of the state. And third, sometimes they cause things to happen; that is, they bring about the state of affairs that they represent. This theory of intentionality is an especially attractive way to explain the relationship between thoughts and actions in the construction of an argument about context and the use people make of information.

The structure of behavior, in Searle's analysis, can be accounted for by a set of principles which should explain both the mental and physical aspects of action. These principles can be summarized by eight points.

1. Actions characteristically consist of two components, a mental component and a physical component.

2. The mental component is an intention.

3. The kind of causation which is essential to both the structure of action and the explanation of action is intentional causation.

4. In the theory of actions there are those which are premeditated, which are a result of some kind of planning in advance, and those actions which are spontaneous, where we do something without any prior reflection.

5. The formation of prior intention is, at least generally, the result of practical reasoning. Practical reasoning is always reasoning about how best to decide between conflicting desires.

6. The explanation of an action must have the same content as was in the person's head when he performed the action or when he reasoned toward his intention to perform the action. If the explanation is really explanatory, the content that causes behavior by way of intentional causation must be identical with the content in the explanation of the behavior.

7. Any intentional state only functions as part of a network of other intentional states. Functions determine their conditions of satisfaction relative to a whole lot of other intentional states. Furthermore, our mental states only function in the way they do because they function against a background of capacities, abilities, skills, habits, ways of doing things, and general stances toward the world that do not themselves consist in intentional states.

8. The whole network of intentionality only functions against a background of human capacities that are not in themselves mental states.

Mental and physical actions, however, exist within contexts which we can analyze in much the same way as we might analyze individuals. Without the organization, the intentions cannot be discerned and without the structure in which a classification can be done, there can never be any criteria of adequacy.

Let us apply this to a common sort of situation. When you see that I am walking out of the room you can suppose all kinds of things about my intentionality. You might think that I am on my way to get a drink of water, and there might be good reasons to suppose so. But I could claim that my intention is to walk to the pizzeria. The act of walking is the physical component of my action, the intention is my idea of going to the pizzeria (1, 2). Intentional causation links them together (3), and the action is premeditated (4). I have gone through some sort of practical reasoning to conclude that I should go to the pizzeria (5), and I am able to explain, or at least articulate in some way my thinking (6). My intention to go to the pizzeria is linked to other intentional states, such as my fondness for pizza and my capacity to walk there (7), and all the elements of this action exist within the context of innumerable human capacities (8).

Now we can make the move from our understanding of the structure of behavior to a more analytical approach to communication.

Speech acts

Any specimen of communication uses language and involves a linguistic act. In the act of speaking we produce symbols which constitute the basic units of linguistic communication. For this reason we need to take into consideration much more than the production of a word to understand the communication of information; we need to perform an analysis which encompasses the whole speech act. Similarly, for an understanding of an information system, we need to know more than the symbols which are being communicated. Searle developed speech act analysis to the point where we can begin to use it in analyzing the pragmatic character of a system.

Central to Searle's notion is that intentionality makes the difference between an incomprehensible noise and a comprehensible one. A further issue is that the performance of such things as speech acts is to engage in a rule-governed form of behavior. We can identify a set of necessary and sufficient conditions for the performance of a particular kind of act. Then we can extract from those conditions a set of rules for using the expressions and identify the utterance as an act of that specific kind.

What, then, are these sorts of rules? We must distinguish between different kinds of rules. These are rules which regulate existing forms of behavior. For example, the rules of etiquette regulates interpersonal relationships, but these relationships exist independently of the rule of etiquette. However, some rules do not merely regulate but create or define new forms of behavior. So we can distinguish between **regulative** rules and **constitutive** rules. Regulative rules generally have the form "do x," or "if y do x." Some members of the set of constitutive rules have a similar form but some also have the form "x counts as y." We can perhaps begin to see why in analyzing intentions the most interesting issues take the form of constitutive rules. A language can be regarded as a series of systems of constitutive rules and speech acts are performed in accordance with these sets of constitutive rules.

Let us look at Searle's example of analyzing the act of promising. First we must consider what the necessary and sufficient conditions are to determine whether an act of promising has been performed in a particular uttered sentence. We can identify a set of propositions which, taken together, specify that a speaker made a promise. It has to work the other way, too, so that the proposition that the speaker made a promise is the result of the conjunction of that set. Therefore, each condition will be a necessary condition for the performance of the act of promising and, taken collectively, the set of conditions will be a sufficient condition for the act to have been performed.

Before we go ahead and construct that set, we have to exclude cases which are odd, deviant, or borderline. This form of analysis is not very robust and cannot deal with partially defective cases, such as those made by an elliptical turn of phrase, hints, or metaphors. In other words, we must recognize that this analytical approach cannot construct strict rules which might take care of every real life condition. The limitations of a rule based system should be recognized from the outset.

So here is how we specify the conditions which constitute the rules for promising within a speech act:

1. Normal input and output conditions obtain.

This rule is intended to cover the conditions such as the use of a mutually intelligible language, that the conditions of communication are not extraordinary, and that those involved in the communication are prepared seriously to cope with the kind of speech acts to follow.

2. The speaker expresses that a promise is made in the utterance of the sentence. Phrases such as "I promise," or "I give you my word that I will," should be used.

This condition isolates the propositional content from the rest of the speech act.

3. In expressing that promise, the speaker predicates a future act of the speaker.

Conditions 2 and 3 are called propositional content conditions because they deal with the substance of promising.

4. The hearer would prefer the speaker to do the act and the speaker believes that the hearer would prefer his doing the act to his not doing the act.

5. It is not obvious to both the speaker and hearer that the speaker will do the act in the normal course of events.

Conditions 4 and 5 are called preparatory conditions. They identify the expectations of the people involved.

6. The speaker intends to do the act.

This is referred to as the condition of sincerity.

7. The speaker intends that the utterance of the sentence will place him or her under an obligation to do the act.

This is the essential condition and secures the intention to comply.

8. The speaker intends that the utterance of the sentence will produce in the hearer a belief that conditions 6 and 7 obtain by means of the recognition of the intention to produce that belief, and he intends this recognition to be achieved by means of the recognition of the sentence as one conventionally used to produce such beliefs.

This might be regarded as a part of condition 1, but it further explains what is meant by the act of being serious.

9. The semantical rules of the dialect spoken by the speaker and hearer are such that the sentence is correctly and sincerely uttered if and only if conditions 1-8 obtain.

Conditions 8 and 9, as well as 1, apply generally to all kinds of normal speech acts and are not peculiar to promising, so rules for the analysis of promising are to be found corresponding to rules 2-7. These rules then need corresponding rules for the application of the analysis.

1. A promise is to be uttered only in the context of a sentence, the utterance of which predicates some future act of the speaker.

This is a propositional content rule derived from propositional content conditions 2 and 3.

2. A promise is to be uttered only if the hearer would prefer the speaker to do the act to his not doing the act, and the speaker believes the hearer would prefer the speaker to do the act to not doing it.

3. A promise is to be uttered only if it is not obvious to both the speaker and the hearer that the speaker will do the act in the normal course of events.

Rules 2 and 3 are preparatory rules and are derived from the preparatory conditions 4 and 5.

4. A promise is to be uttered only if the speaker intends to do the act.

This is the sincerity rule, derived from the sincerity condition 6.

5. The utterance of the promise counts as the undertaking of an obligation to do the act.

These rules are ordered: rules 2-5 apply only if rule 1 is satisfied, and rule 5 applies only if rules 2 and 3 are satisfied as well. Furthermore, rules 1-4 take on the form of quasi-imperatives, that is, they take the form: utter the promise only if x. Rule 5 takes the form: the utterance of the promise counts as y.

Let us apply this in a shorter form to another speech act: that of denying. Since condition rule 1 is general we can start of specific application with rule 2, which requires us to use some phrase such as "I deny," or "I didn't do it." This must refer to a supposed earlier act of the speaker (3), and the hearer must be someone who might believe that the speaker did the act and the speaker should believe that by saying he denies it that the hearer could be convinced (4). It cannot be obvious to the speaker and the hearer that in the normal course of events they can assume that the speaker did not do the act (5), and the speaker should believe that he did not do the act (6). Additionally, the speaker should believe that the utterance of the phrase will oblige him to stand behind his denial (7). Condition rules 8 and 9 are general so we do not need to specify them further.

Now we must use these rules with the correspondence rules to complete the analysis. Rule 1 indicates that the denial uttered in the context of a sentence is part of a reference to a supposed previous act. Rule 2 indicates that the denial should be uttered only if the hearer is susceptible to being convinced of the falseness of the accusation, and the speaker believes this is possible; furthermore, it should not be obvious (rule 3). The speaker must be sincere in the denial (rule 4) and he must understand that the uttering of the statement will oblige him to stand behind his denial (5).

Speech act analysis gives us an opportunity to see in great detail how the pragmatic character of a situation can be understood. We can see how a careful analysis of the speech acts in a conversation can provide us with an understanding of the intentionality of the participants. Although this form of analysis is too cumbersome to recommend in every case, it is useful to be able to perform when the occasion demands. For the pizzeria, "ordering" is a vital act, and it may be worthwhile to examine in great detail what the necessary and sufficient conditions are.

By studying the pragmatic properties of signs, we can understand the cultural and contextual framework within which communication takes place. This gives us a firm basis on which to build an approach to the semantic properties of signs.

Discussion issues

1. Is the notion of the thought community viable for analyzing problems of information systems?

2. Divide the class into two or more distinct cultural groups. Each group should devise a sub-language for giving directions for moving around locally. Compare your results and analyze the reasons for the differences which emerge.

3. Why is it necessary to assume that people have purposeful behavior? If we are not convinced that people have purposes which are non-random, how can we analyze their use of information?

4. Identify the norms which govern behavior in your library. Separate those which are decreed by the institution from those which are informal.

5. Analyze the speech act of "requesting" in the context of seeking access to a confidential student record file.

6. Compare the speech acts of "confirming" and "ordering" (as in ordering a pizza).

Exercises

1. Construct a scenario where a group of people with no previous connection come to form a thought community. Give examples of how otherwise faulty information can be correctly interpreted because of shared assumptions.

2. Show how E.T. Hall's streams of cultural messages can be applied to a club or association to which you belong.

3. Using the method of J. R. Searle, analyze the speech act of apologizing.

4. Create an outline for perceptual norms analogous to the Inuit [Eskimo] variety of terms used to describe snow, which will distinguish among the different tactile gradations of coarseness in sweaters.

5. Analyze the grading system used in your institution in terms of evaluative norms. Compare that system with the one used in your high school.

6. Why do all groups use norms? Discuss the relationship between context and norms.

Suggested reading

Bloor, David, *Knowledge and Social Imagery*, London: RKP, 1976.
An argument built from the mainstream of thought in the sociology of knowledge, applied to concepts of science and leading to the presentation of the "Strong Program" for the sociology of scientific knowledge.

Douglas, Mary, *How Institutions Think*, Syracuse: Syracuse University Press, 1986.
A synthesis of Douglas's writings, most usefully applied to institutions of various kinds, educational, commercial, political. At its root is a moralistic argument based on the notion that "for better or worse, individuals really do share their thoughts and they do to some extent harmonize their preferences, and they have no other way to make the big decisions except within the scope of institutions they build."

Levinson, Stephen C., *Pragmatics*, Cambridge Textbooks in Linguistics, Cambridge: Cambridge University Press, 1983.
One of a useful series of textbooks which covers in great detail the linguistic aspects of concepts of pragmatics.

John R. Searle, *Minds, Brains and Science*, Cambridge, Mass.: Harvard University Press, 1986.
Based on the popular Reith Lectures of the British Broadcasting Corporation, this collection of essays takes the reader from the concept of cognition through arguments about whether computers can think, to an explanation of intentionality.

4 Semantics

- *Meaning*
- *Semantic problems*
- *Schema*
- *Semantic analysis*

Once we are able to understand the context of communication, we must confront the problem of its meaning. Only after we are able to analyze the meaning of acts of communication can we begin to build complete information systems. In all cases we must consider what information we need and analyze its significance. Semantics is the study of what signs refer to. By devising **schema** we can reveal the semantic structure of a social situation. Further specification can be achieved when we apply the techniques of **semantic analysis**.

For information systems, where organizations use language and other systems of signs to perform their business tasks, the semantics of the signs processed, stored and interpreted into action are fundamental to the success of the enterprise. Managers use signs, primarily language, to direct the activities of their staff. Using signs effectively means that no time will be wasted in pursuing the prime task of business. In complex business environments the potential problems of misunderstandings are so great that they consume a huge proportion of the effort expended in internal communication. Consider the amount of time that business people typically spend in meetings. Most of that time is devoted to agreeing on meanings.

The semantic properties of signs can only be investigated once the context of their use has been determined. We have seen how, in Chapter 3, understanding the setting in which signs are used is crucial to the success of communication. After the context is known, we may begin to address the semantics in an information system. Experience shows us that there are many problems in organizations that owe their origin to semantic ambiguity. When different people place different meanings on key terms used, then misunderstandings will lead to difficulties for the business.

Meaning

The communication of intentions involves the use and interpretation of signs. When we communicate, we use signs which have to be interpreted. When we present our intentions to others we go through a process of externalizing; that is, we choose signs, usually linguistic ones, which embody for us our intentions.

Can we assume that once we are able to talk about something, using words which seem appropriate, we are giving meaning to our statements? Can we be sure that the meanings we attribute to those words will be the same for the person to whom we are speaking? These concerns are closely allied to the problems associated with the construction of information systems, to the question of how data becomes information, and indeed to whether computers can interpret knowledge. However, no matter which concern is addressed, the problem remains that we need to understand the process of relating signs to their referents, the things they refer to.

One approach is to examine the problem as one of understanding how a person interprets a sign so that it can become knowledge. This is a conceptual approach, where the concern about making meaning stops at the point at which the interpreter has made sense of the sign by intellectual activity. There are many theories about how an individual translates signs into knowledge, rooted in the fields of philosophy and psycholinguistics. An alternative approach considers the question up to the point where some action or behavior results from that interpretation. Our concern is to understand how signs are used to get things done in organizations. This understanding may come from the use of an explicit theory, or from applying metaphors that are used every day, often unconsciously.

We can find metaphors which express how information is obtained from signs. Rather than having an explicit theory, we use these metaphors to explain how this works. One example is the "brain as computer" metaphor where the activity of the brain is seen as the input, processing and output of signs, just like a computer. Apart from the unflattering comparison of human intelligence with the work of a machine, the metaphor treats the interpretation of signs as trivial, something that any computer can do. The human interpretation of signs is portrayed as parallel to the logical manipulations of symbols performed by the processor in a computer. But whereas a person can translate the signs received into their referents in the world of actions, the computer can only transpose one set of signs, or symbols, into another set. The computer remains firmly fixed in the realm of signs.

Another metaphor, found in the definition of information by H.D. Clifton in Chapter 1, is that of information as some mystical fluid extracted from data by a process of distillation. This chemical engineering metaphor sees information, or data with meanings, as something achieved through processing. Once this fluid has been distilled, it presumably can be bottled, or pumped around in pipes, and sent to where it is needed. We have little idea from this of how the data acquire their meanings. Will the distillation process always give the same results with the same data? What is the role in this process of making meaning for the people using this information in their daily business?

We only find explicit theories about semantics when we go through the process of analysis. One approach to semantics is that of naming and meaning. Here the problem of meaning is seen as the problem of reference, and therefore how words name things. In this naming and meaning approach, proper nouns name objects, common nouns name sets of objects, verbs name actions, prepositions name relations, while adjectives and adverbs name properties of objects and actions. Up to a point, names do allow us to identify things in the world. Complex concepts, however, begin to give problems. When we name things we rely on the name referring to something unique. That uniqueness begins to give us problems when there are legitimate alternative meanings for common words, or where the expression of a complex idea requires us either to refer to it in very elaborate terms, or run the risk of its being commonly misinterpreted.

In our pizzeria, the regular customers will know that the "Four Seasons" pizza comes with capers, olives, onions, and anchovies. Their guests might expect four different toppings, or assume that they will get pepperoni instead of anchovies because that is how it is done at their local place. The mistake is a common form of misapprehension about the difference between naming and meaning, in so far as the title has been altered. The type of pizza might be a "Four Seasons," but the one our customers are waiting for is not properly identified by that title. Another aspect of the naming/meaning problem occurs when our diners decide that one of the pizzas should be extra crispy. The waiter will return with two similar pizzas, but here again we have a problem with the general name, because "Four Seasons" does not distinguish crispiness. Further communication is needed to specify which is which.

The problem quickly becomes much more complex when we begin to deal with concepts whose individuality is impossible to define. Such social abstractions do not specify unique conditions such as the start and finish of an act. Let us question whether our diners are satisfied with their dinner.

The word "satisfaction" is a term that refers to an abstract concept. How can we know that the satisfaction they express is with the dinner, rather than something else, such as the occasion in general. The smiles on their faces may be pleasure in each other's company, or the success of the birthday celebration that the dinner has marked. The chef may think that their joy is over his mastery of the pizza oven; only an insider will know the specific cause of their satisfaction.

When we apply a theory of meaning, it should allow us to take signs and consistently come to know the thing or concept to which it refers. This helps us to overcome the confusion created by distinctions such as between a concept and an occurrence of that concept, as with the "Four Seasons" pizza. Similarly, we can reduce the confusion caused by the label and the unique object to which it refers in a particular instance, as with the crispy versus the regular pizza. Names may be labels, but they do not necessarily direct us to the unique object.

As a basis for semantics, naming and meaning is unsatisfactory. It does not provide an exhaustive and consistent explanation of meaning for all the terms that we want to use in discourse. Communicating well requires us to supply consistently the appropriate signification of any signs that are employed. If in social exchanges different significations are given then communication breakdown will result.

Semantic problems

Semantic problems arise wherever people use a system of signs or symbols and these signs have to be translated into the world of action. In a game of computer chess we do not have to interpret the significance of the battle between the "armies" of the two players, although the game is modelled on military encounters. Chess pieces stand for themselves and the game has no external significance. However, when a bank manipulates signs on the bank statement of one of its customers then those signs do have a significance beyond the symbolic world. It is crucial that there is agreement between the bank and the customer about what those signs refer to. The customer must understand that figures in one column imply debits rather than credits, otherwise there could be unfortunate consequences. What matters is not how the customer translates these signs into mental notions, but rather what actions ensue.

The more complex, physically distant and culturally diverse the parties involved in communication, the more problems are likely to emerge because of confusion. The sources of that confusion are found chiefly in the double sided nature of using signs and making sense of them.

Our pizzeria uses a menu with glossy photographs of their pizzas. We all know that such pictures are meant to represent the food we hope to get. But in some cases customers might complain that the pizza they were served was different from the one they ordered because it did not look the same to them as the photograph. If we order an anchovy pizza where in the photograph the anchovies are clearly on top of the melted mozzarella, and we can not see them on our pizza, then we might point to the picture and tell the waiter that he brought us the wrong pizza. His response might be to say, "No, it's the same," and to point to some anchovies buried in the cheese on our pizza. This little problem arose because there were different interpretations of what the picture referred to. We interpreted the picture as a literal representation of the pizza we were going to be served, while the waiter understood that the picture referred to any pizza with anchovies on it.

"*THAT'S NOT THE ONE!*"

Take the apparently simple question of counting the buildings that a big company uses. The type of structures might range from skyscrapers to shacks, with all kinds of other things in between. But what counts as a building? The accounts department uses a criterion based on the values of structures as they depreciate over their useful life. For them, cheap shacks would not count, radio towers would, and new annexes to larger buildings would be regarded as separate from the older parts. The legal department would include any structure that the company owns, so annexes would not be considered as separate, but shacks and towers would be buildings. The space allocation committee is interested in any useful office area, so neither towers nor shacks count, and annexes are included with the structures to which they are attached.

Distance can be an important complicating factor, too. Consider the case of a lawyer in New York acting on behalf of an absentee landlord in California who wants him to check the appropriateness of potential commercial tenants. For the lawyer, the range of appropriate tenants would include any business able to pay the rent and to comply with zoning laws. If a chemical company wishes to rent the building, then the lawyer would see no problem. The landlord, however, might prefer a cleaner and safer tenant and he might object. If they had been together there would have been less chance of any misinterpretation of the meaning of "appropriate."

These problems are further complicated when cultural differences intervene. If a multinational corporation decides that each subsidiary will hold early morning briefings, this policy will hinge on the meaning of "early." In a country where office hours begin at 9:30 am, an early morning briefing is not the same as a breakfast meeting.

Consider the problems which might arise within a family. The head of the family might normally demand that a teenager be home by midnight and say: "Be sure to be back on time," accompanied by a wink. The wink could easily be interpreted either as an accompanying emphasis to the bland spoken part of the message, or it might indicate something exceptional. For example, an exception might be in the mind of the sender which indicates that overstaying on this occasion would be acceptable. The wink could then be interpreted as a contrary indication, meaning approximately, "Enjoy yourself and don't worry too much this time about the rules." This could be a problem even in the closest family where there are many shared assumptions and a great deal of understanding. The semantic content is seen to be understood only when the teenager is fully aware of the intentions of the head of the family.

For most face-to-face contact, problems of communication can be overcome by use of the full range of conscious and sub-conscious devices that people have developed over millennia of collective social activity. At close quarters the physical and logical characteristics of signs, for example the volume of sound and the use of grammar, may be less important. Indeed at the informal level we can concentrate on resolving problems of intention and meaning. The social control of language, exercised through informal norms, assures that use of the language in a given social context is consistent. For newcomers to a place of work, the meaning of the terms employed in that context will become clear as the process of assimilation into that sub-culture advances. They will learn through their daily experience an operational definition of, for example, punctuality. Transgressions will be punished through the exercise of norms. Equally, for the errant offspring who know that their parents want them in by dusk, the years of close physical contact have made sure that the intention and meaning of the signs employed in the doorstep conversation prior to setting out for the day are well understood. In that case, any refusal to comply is not a communication problem but a conflict of wills.

Signs do not carry around with them inherent meanings. A sign can mean whatever those using it choose it to mean, and the same sign may have several meanings depending upon the context. As interpreters of signs in many different contexts we have learned a battery of different possible interpretations, only one of which will be appropriate in any situation. The problem is to find the right interpretation at any given moment. And yet despite all these possible misunderstandings, people do seem to communicate perfectly well most of the time. There has to be common agreement about meaning. This common agreement is generally not arrived at by some deliberate process of negotiation, but instead is embodied in the cultural conventions and norms of the social context. We learn from participating in a given social context what particular signs refer to. Acting on the assumption that meanings are objective, although attractive because of the sense of security it gives, is dangerously misleading.

For analytical work in information problems, it is useful to be able to build a framework of the signs used in any organizational context and so to understand the semantics of these signs. There is no way to resolve the problem of ambiguity and the confusions which arise unless we have an adequate understanding of the way signs are used in organizations.

We can begin to find solutions to these problems by taking an analytical approach. In setting about the task of analyzing how signs take on meaning we can use the work of the philosopher Charles Morris. For him the problem of meaning had to be tackled from a larger perspective:

> The basic terms of semiotic can be introduced as follows: Semiosis (or sign process) is regarded as a five-term relation -v, w, x, y, z- in which v sets up in w the disposition to react in a certain kind of way, x, to a certain kind of object y (not then acting as a stimulus), under certain conditions, z. The v's, in the cases where this relation obtains, are *signs*, the w's are *interpreters*, the x's are the *interpretants*, the y's are *significations*, and the z's are the *contexts* in which the signs occur.

This approach shows us one way of interpreting common signs and their associated meanings.

Take the example of the dance of the bees, where a bee which finds nectar on returning to the hive "dances" in such a way as to direct the other bees to the food source. In this case the dance is the sign (v); the other bees are the interpreters (w); the disposition to react in a certain way is the interpretant (x); and the kind of object toward which the bees are prepared to react in this way is the signification of the sign (y); and the position of the hive is the context (z).

Notice that the disposition to act in a particular way does not amount to the commission of the act itself. While the bees may be intent upon returning to the spot where the nectar lies, there may be many circumstances which could confound them in their attempts, such as a sudden wind. It is important also to note that the word "meaning" does not appear in his exposition. Morris suggests avoiding the term entirely for discussions of semiotics, or else using the word to refer to both signification and interpretant and neither alone. For this example, the type of flowers indicated by the dance and the readiness of the other bees to react in a particular way towards them, together amount to the "meaning" of the sign.

This analytical method can be applied to all signs in any context. Take for example the use of a "No Smoking" sign in an office. The notice on the wall is the sign, and in this case will probably be the common sign of the red slash over a lighted cigarette. The interpreters of this sign will be any persons in the office for whatever reason: clerical staff, cleaners, members of the public. The interpretant of the sign is the readiness or disposition to abstain from smoking, while the signification is refraining from smoking. The office provides the context, and outside that area the sign does not apply to these people.

What is crucially different here from commonly held notions of meaning is the rejection of the idea of an intrinsic meaning to a sign, and its replacement by a model which relies upon two agents or groups interacting in a complex exchange whose effectiveness is tested in the actual behavior of the parties involved. We have to identify the context of the sign, the agents who will interpret it, the effect on their behavioral intentions, and how they might behave.

Schema

In an organization we generally find the same terms being used over and over again. These terms are sometimes referred to as the **universe of discourse**. This universe contains all the terms which people use when participating in those surroundings. In an airline the terms "passenger," "seat," "flight," and "booking," will recur constantly. For those who work in this industry, being able to use these terms with precision is vital. For those building information systems in this area it is just as important.

We need a means of setting up the conditions within which we can use tools. This we do by building what we call a **schema**. A schema is a framework or structure for all the terms in any universe of discourse. We can see from the schema what relationships prevail between the terms and so reveal the semantic structures. Although the concept of schema is of special use to us for analyzing semantics, it originated in the analysis and design of computer databases, where you need to have a schema of all the data used in the organization. In a database, a schema is the structure within which the business defines and stores its data values. Without that structure the business cannot keep track of the changing values in its domain. In a sense the schema is a model of the universe of the business.

To design a schema we need to understand the domain because it must embody knowledge about the conditions and elements of the situation. The structure of our pizzeria can be specified as a schema. The first thing we would want to do in developing a schema would be to identify all the key signs associated with the business. We would discover these signs in the discourse we engage in when we enter into the situation. The signs would include such terms as:

person	waiter
eats	purchases
pizza	owes
pizzeria	orders
owns	debtor
manager	creditor
cook	customer

To construct a schema, we take such terms and apply our concept of the semantic content of the situation. Let us first clarify the structure and re-cast these activities in the form of a story, or description of a typical situation. This allows us to set a context of use, from which we can base the meanings employed for the terms. A customer comes into the restaurant and orders a pizza. The staff take the order and proceed to make the pizza. When ready, the pizza is served to the customer's table, whereupon the customer (presuming the pizza looks ok) begins to eat. After having eaten, the customer pays and receives change.

Now, let us turn these agents, objects and events into a structure which will allow us to record instances of these things when they are realized. To begin with, we can see that there are a number of agents who have roles in certain relationships in these activities. There are persons who order pizzas (customers), who eat pizzas (consumers), who owe money before settling debts (debtors) and who own the establishment (proprietor). The pizzeria is a business entity that is comprised of several positions, such as cook, waiter, and manager. These positions comprise the organizational structure and will usually outlast the occupancy of the particular persons holding down the positions, so that cooks will come and go, but the position of cook remains. Here we have separated these positions as elements of the business organization from the roles that people occupy in the course of performing an action.

In analyzing this universe of discourse we discover that the person who eats the pizza will not always be the person who has a right to it, so that the schema should distinguish between these two. Neither does the order have to come from either of these two, for it might be ordered by a third party. The person who orders the pizzas performs a communication act which requires the use of a sign, perhaps a gesture to the waiter or a more formal directive with the waiter taking a note of it. The sign refers to the purchase of the ownership of the pizza, and is used in the act of ordering.

Semantic analysis

The construction of a schema requires the analysis of the semantic content of a situation. We call this analytical process **semantic analysis**. Semantic analysis uses a set of symbols to reveal the basis upon which the terms take on meaning. To develop our schema we find the people and things within the system, the **agents** and **entities**. The first step would be to take the list of terms used for creating a schema and underline the agents, those terms which refer to those who can take responsibility for actions. In the case of the pizzeria we can identify the customer, staff and cook. These terms, however, are role names and we must go beyond names to identify their particular activity. For example, the concept of customer might apply to people when they walk into the pizzeria, or it might be restricted to the point at which they have a debt to pay. We are looking for relationships among agents. That already begins to direct us to some structure. So here, the notion of "owns" will be a relationship between a pizzeria and a legal person. Taking these elements together, we can begin to construct our structure.

The basic symbols used in semantic analysis are those which show the relationships between agents and entities. In addition, we can record a small amount of information about the character of these agents, entities and relationships.

——	line of existence dependency
#	hash sign for individuals
( )	brackets for role names
" "	Speech mark for signs used in speech acts
- - - - - -	dotted line for referent of signs
•	period for part/whole relationship

generic   box for generic/specific relationships

generic
specific 1
specific 2

Symbols used for semantic analysis

1. The hash sign [#] indicates an individual, the singular occurrence of an element. We use it when we can pick out an individual; something we could not do when we described the concept of satisfaction. For example, people can be singled out as persons, or we can pick out the pizzeria as a business.

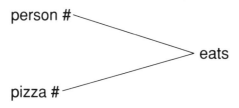

2. The line which indicates what has to exist shows that what is to its right depends on what is to its left. In other words, the right one is contingent upon the left one. For example, we can not realize the eating of a pizza without the contingent elements: a pizza and a person. These two symbols can be simply illustrated.

3. The point [•] is placed on a line between two entities to show that the entity to the right is a part of the entity to the left. For example, the staff form part of the structure of the business.

4. Brackets [( )] indicate a name which specifies a role that an entity plays in a relationship with another entity. There are role names for persons, such as creditor and payee, and for things, such as responsibility and property. These indicate roles within relationships and the role names apply only while the relationship exists.

5. Quotation marks [" "] enclose a sign which is used to refer to some entity when agents communicate. For example, when a person orders a pizza, they will say, "one pizza, please." Terms in quotation marks are signs used to get things done in the business. In this process the signs we are interested in are those involved in communication acts. We are not interested in the signs that record changes in the state of the affairs of the business, such as the books that the proprietor might keep, but in the signs that are used to effect changes in social and legal commitments, such as in the process of ordering food.

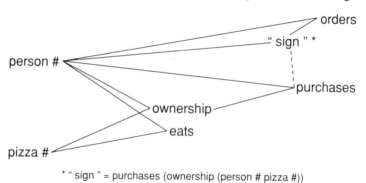

* " sign " = purchases (ownership (person # pizza #))

Section of schema for ordering a pizza

This diagram tells us that a person can have ownership of a pizza, can eat a pizza, can purchase the ownership, and can order a pizza using some sign. The person in each case may be different.

6. A dotted line [. . . . .] shows what is being referred to, so that in ordering a pizza a person must make use of a sign that signifies the existence of the purchase of a pizza, or more accurately the transfer of the ownership of the pizza from the proprietor to the customer. This sign might be a waving of the hand by a regular customer whose requirements are well known.

7. A box indicates a generic/specific relationship where the specifics are listed inside the box and the generic is written on top of the box. On the staff there

are positions that are filled by persons from time to time. The generic is "position" and the specifics are "manager," "cook," "waiter" and so on.

Only one of the terms shown on the diagram on the next page, "Echo Pizza," is a particular, that is, the rest do not refer to any particular manager or pizza that has an existence. Instead they are universals and refer to what may exist in this universe at any time. If we build a database using this schema, then the particulars will be reflected by the data values we store inside the computer to represent something in the business: values for particular persons such as their names, addresses and so on.

Although this approach is conceptually related to the process of modelling databases, it provides us with greater stability by having more rigor. Here we are not limited, as with many database models, to simplistic relationships established by guesswork. Part of the advantage is that we have a way of eliciting knowledge which uncovers semantic ambiguities. For example, there may be different views about which person is the customer. Is it the person who steps into the pizzeria, who orders the pizza, who eats the pizza, or who pays the bill? The resolution of this ambiguity could have significant implications for how the business organizes itself, for these are all roles that "customers" enter into when coming to eat, but they may not be played by the same persons.

For each term we enter into the schema we must find (1) what the criteria are for starting and finishing the occurrence of the particular, (2) who is the agent who determines when something has been realized, and (3) what has to exist to allow for this occurrence.

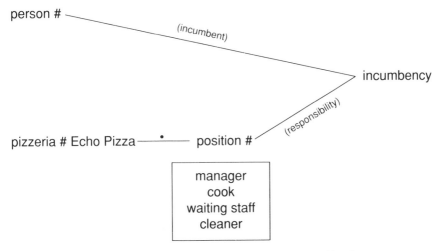

Section of schema showing staff positions as part of business

For the starting and finishing criteria, we might consider the incumbency by a person of a role. By incumbency we refer to the occupying of a position in some organization, and the taking of certain responsibilities. For example, the pizzeria needs to work out precisely under what conditions a person can be said to be a manager. When the person ends their period in that post the precise conditions for establishing the finish of the incumbency should be found. Such analysis would resolve any ambiguities about whose responsibility it was to secure the premises, and at what point that responsibility ceased, so that in the event of a robbery the person responsible for locking up can be identified.

We need to know who the responsible agent is for determining when something exists. It may be that a regular customer who lives in the building opposite the pizzeria has occasionally tried to signal his order by gesticulating from the window. Who decides what constitutes an order for the business? Will it be the waiters, the manager, or even the cook? We may draw up rules to cover such things, but ultimately we will have to point to a person who will apply them.

Looking at the part of the schema for the purchase of pizza, we can see, for example, that an incumbency of a post by a person can not commence until the person exists and the business exists. We are able to use this diagram to see what is possible at any particular point, and what is necessary. Moving from left to right on our pizzeria schema, we can see what is possible in the world of the pizzeria; whereas moving in the opposite direction we can see what is necessary. So that in order to have a person who "purchases," reading from right to left, it is necessary to have a "person" and an "ownership," that of a pizza from the pizzeria. Starting from the left and reading to the right, we can see the possibility of a particular "purchase," at a particular price ("$").

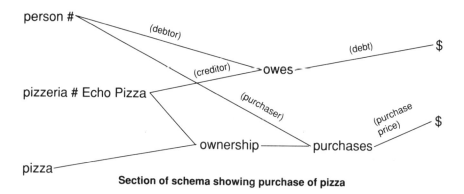

Section of schema showing purchase of pizza

This kind of analysis leads quickly to questions about the business policies of our restaurant. For example, what should constitute a sign that the business will accept as appropriate for an order is a critical question for the business to resolve. Are we going to take telephone orders? Do we need some special identification, such as a telephone number? Are we going to limit our telephone ordering service for known, regular customers?

This approach is generally useful for simple situations, but larger problems can be dealt with in the same way. We are able to allow our diagrams to become somewhat more elaborate. For example, if we wish to take into consideration the complexity of the relationship between the customer and the business, we may want to specify when pizzas are charged for. The relationship which describes purchasing could be said to involve a variety of different activities, such as owing money from a person to a business. The person who owes has the role of debtor. The agent who is owed the money is the creditor. These roles persist until the debt is paid. By this means we can separate the two notions of incurring a debt and purchasing. This allows the schema to cover a much wider range of contexts. Paying some money changes the value of the amount owed and perhaps finishes the debt altogether. the determiners ($) for "purchases" and for "owes" would be a numerical value for which we may use the terms "purchase price" and "debt." This does not require the sum which is paid to be the sum which is owed. Often, debtors pay some amount other than the actual debt. Consider the common practice of paying a portion of a credit card bill. Your debt is not deleted, but you have paid (a part of) the bill. A new value for debt outstanding exists and the old one is finished.

These constraints assure that our semantic analysis takes us to the very roots of the business problem and the resulting schema reflects behavior in that context. It provides us with an operational definition of meaning. From the schema we can discern what operations have to be performed to bring anything into existence, because of the time constraints. The power of this technique rests entirely on the base built by a coherent theory of meaning. Only when we are confident that we know where that theory of meaning stands in relation to the broader context of activities, the pragmatics of the situation, can we make full use of it. And only when we are able to link it to the other elements of the total system of signs, including syntax and empirics, can we construct a full system. In the semiotic framework, the semantics of any signs used in discourse need to be established before analyzing the logical validity of the expressions uttered and the physical transmission of signals. If we do not know the meaning of the terms we use, then our knowledge of the grammar of a language is of little value.

Discussion issues

1. Divide the class into two groups each of which should produce a schema
    using semantic analysis on the following problems:
    a) A newspaper delivery job involves picking up the papers at a central
    location and distributing them at front doors in the neighborhood. Each
    customer needs to be invoiced monthly and payment is accepted only in
    cash.
    b) A record needs to be kept of hobbyists in a club. As club secretary,
    you want to be able to contact all members effectively. You want to build
    a database which will allow you to contact people at their places of work,
    at home, or through the nearest neighboring member.

2. Discuss the perspectives presented on pages 3 - 5. Consider the metaphors
    for information which are implicit and reveal alternative concepts of the
    semantic nature of information.

3. Using the symbols of semantic analysis, draw up a diagram for a small
    problem area of your own choice. Give it to another student without
    revealing the story behind your diagram. Discuss the effectiveness of the
    method of representation and show how your diagram can be improved
    after taking into consideration any confusion which has arisen.

4. Apply Charles Morris's classification in the theory of signs to animals
    other than bees which make use of signs in a similar way. For instance,
    foxes urinating around their territory; chameleons changing their color;
    roosters raising their combs; birdsong.

5. Discuss how ambiguity in the use of terms such as "good," "late," "quick"
    are resolved in normal circumstances.

6. Take the role of a manager who needs to standardize the usage of the
    terms "good quality," "late delivery," "quick service." Discuss the problem
    of imposing these standards.

Exercises

1. Consider the scenario of a diversified company with many departments: accounts, legal, marketing, advertising, retail division, procurement. Each of them uses the term "customer" in the course of its work. The business is considering setting up a company-wide database for all its operations, and the different departments will use the database when exchanging information. Anticipate the semantic problems; discuss how to resolve them.

2. Consider the parallels of territorial disputes within a family, between two subsidiaries of a multinational corporation, and two neighboring countries. After drawing up details of each dispute, analyze the semantic content and comment on the limitations of any universal meaning of the concept of territoriality.

3. Identify in the following examples, the five terms in Charles Morris's five term relation:
   traffic lights turning red
   hailing a taxi in New York or London
   getting the attention of a waiter
   a wedding ceremony
   the inauguration of a president

4. Categorize the following list into sets of things which have legs and things which are living: amoeba, cat, chair, desk, horse, snail, snake, spider, table, tripod. Since these are not discrete categories, discuss how to resolve the problem of grouping them.

5. List 10 different kinds of built structures. How do you decide which should be called buildings?

6. Write an essay on the effect of the move away from printed media to electronic documentation on the problem of semantics. Consider especially the difference that mass dissemination makes.

Suggested reading

Aitchison, Jean, *Words in the Mind*, Oxford: Blackwell, 1988.
Humans manage to recall enormous numbers of words. This text examines the concept of the mental lexicon, and provides a picture of how it works.

Carroll, John B. (ed.), *Language, Thought and Reality; Selected writings of B.L. Whorf*, Cambridge, Mass.: MIT Press, 1956.
Whorf's writings on linguistics have been very influential. They stress the role of linguistics in the analysis of meaning and thinking. His general hypothesis is that language is a key factor in our understanding of reality and how we behave.

Schank, Roger, *The Cognitive Computer*, Reading, Mass.: Addison-Wesley, 1985.
The inability of computers to have empathy underlines their inherent incapacity to know fully the meaning of anything. Schank develops his theory for the semantic limitations of computers in an interesting and lively way.

Winograd, Terry and Flores, Carlos F., *Understanding Computers and Cognition*, Norwood, N.J.: Ablex, 1987.
The first author of this interesting but difficult book was a pioneer of research into language and artificial intelligence. From the standpoint of cognitive philosophy, this book stresses the limitations of computers in handling problems of meaning and intention.

5 Syntactics

- *Language*
- *Usage and reference*
- *The use and limits of logical analysis*
  propositional logic
  predicate logic
  modal and deontic logics
- *Objectivist vs. subjectivist theories*

In order to construct a complete system we need to be able to take advantage of the means of formalizing the way in which we represent information. By formalizing we provide rigor to the use of language by the constraints of vocabulary, grammar and the rules which govern them. This allows us to construct information systems which have consistency, integrity and validity.

Language

Because language is the central means of expression, we need to be able to use it effectively in the analysis and design of information systems. What, then, constitutes a language? All languages, by definition, consist of a vocabulary, a grammar, and a syntax and, for those which are spoken, phonetics. Vocabulary provides the elements of discourse in the form of terms and is complete for the use of the language. These terms are used in a grammar which controls their use. Syntax provides the formal elements of rules and their operations which allows us to construct sentences. When we use vocabulary, grammar and syntax properly we can express ourselves clearly and expect to be understood.

Languages which we use for everyday communication, such as English or Spanish, are referred to as **natural languages**. All natural languages are highly complex because they reflect the richness of a culture. For this reason linguists study social, psychological, and historical aspects of natural languages.

55

By contrast, **formal languages** are much simpler because they contain only a limited and explicitly defined vocabulary, grammar and syntax. Whereas natural languages are used in everyday communication, formal languages have particular utility for circumstances where precision is necessary.

Since formal languages are artificial, they can be designed specially for specific uses. The most common formalism is the language of mathematics. In algebra, for example, we have a vocabulary of numbers and other symbols; a set of characteristics such as those of associativity, commutivity and transitivity; and rules that govern the ways in which they are used. Similarly, computer programming languages have a vocabulary of terms; a set of operators such as <SELECT>, <AND>, <OR>, and <COUNT>; and rules that govern the construction of programs.

Just as there are different kinds of programming languages which are appropriate for specific tasks, there are different kinds of formalizations. Some serve to simplify complicated situations while others perform difficult logical or mathematical operations. Since logics need to be complete within themselves, no single one can serve every purpose. This can easily be demonstrated by the difference between deductive and inductive inferences. The classic formulation of the difference between a deductive inference and an inductive inference is summarized in the following form:

Deductive Inference

Premises: If it's snowing it's cold
                    It is snowing
Conclusion: It is cold

Inductive Inference

Premises: When it's snowing it's usually cold
                    It is snowing
Conclusion: It is cold

So we can see that the conclusion of an inductive inference is valid only with a certain degree of probability and not necessarily valid, as in the deductive inference. Since most interesting aspects of the study of logic concern deductive inference, there is less consideration given to induction. Induction, however, is of particular interest to us in that it is what we mostly face with so-called "real-life" situations. In conditions where information is incomplete, where decisions need to be made before every last bit of evidence might be gathered, in other words in most common situations, we have to have at least a clear idea of what kind of inference we are dealing with, and the ways in which we can legitimately use induction.

Formality allows us to generalize from particular instances. To generalize is one of the most important functions of any study, and in an approach like the one in this book, it is particularly important to be able to move from theory, to case study, to generalization, and then to application. However, when moving from formality to generalization, syntax alone is not sufficient to be able to understand and express complete ideas.

John Searle's set of principles for the structure of action, as described in Chapter 3, is one explanation of the links between the understanding and expression of ideas in a formal way. This is useful in order to see the basis for decision making and the use of information. Searle's principles for the structure of action provide a bridge between meanings and intentions, and formal representations of language: between semantics and syntax.

Usage and reference

In order to be able to use Searle's ideas for the construction of information systems, we need to relate them to the notions of usage and reference. By usage we mean the ways in which languages, natural or formal, are employed; reference is a concept which links language and action. Once we are able to understand usage and reference we can see how to use a formalism to express semantics and we can provide tools for translating ideas into formalisms for manipulation.

We can use formal language to describe the meanings of expressions in business and information systems by employing logic. One type of formalization has already been introduced in Chapter 4. Semantic analysis uses a logic depicted by lines and nodes. These can express behaviors and norms, and they operate as representations of the meanings in use. Other types of formalization provide tools for representing simple relationships, complex deductions, or extensive quantitative manipulations.

We can observe that when we go through a logical exercise we are **translating**, not just encoding. Part of the reason for this is that the very inflexibility of logic forces us a) to reconceptualize the structure of a text, and b) to use the limited resources of a simplistic grammar of logic in a more "imaginative" way. Some aspects of transforming a text into logical form are indeed like encoding, but there is always the necessity to reconceive of the whole text in order to rectify the form with a natural language grammar.

Logical tools provide the means by which complex situations, instructions and deductions can be represented. That representation is a fundamental step towards systems analysis and encoding.

Consider a typical example of a complex text which is supposed to be logical:

i)   *Student users must not construct or maintain computer files of personal data for use in connection with the academic studies/research without the express authority of an appropriate member of staff.*

ii)   *When giving such authority, the member of staff should make the student aware of the Data Protection Act's requirements, inform them that they must abide by the Data Protection Principles, and of the appropriate level of security arrangements which should attach to a particular set of personal data.*

A number of stages of understanding are needed to decipher such statements:

1. Parse to resolve ambiguity.
2. Assign meanings.
3. Conjure up "images" for these terms.
4. Place these "images" in meaningful relationships to one another.

We should begin by parsing; taking the key terms and identifying what they are and how they are used, as we did with the semantic schema for the pizzeria in Chapter 4.

There are:
students
students who are users
computer files
personal data
academic studies/research
appropriate members of staff
members of staff
Data Protection Act
Data Protection Principles
appropriate level of security
  arrangements
security arrangements

These can be:
constructed
maintained
connected
holding authority
aware
informed
abiding
attached

Next we must assign meanings to these terms so that we can understand how they are used. We might use speech act analysis for some key terms if they are important enough for us, but here we will take a common sense notion of each of them. Thirdly, "images" of entities need to be attached, so we can have not only semantic clarity but also an understanding of the difference between "members of staff" and "appropriate members of staff." Finally, we can put these parts back together, with our deeper understanding of their meanings and relationships. The resultant synthesis might look rather different from the original text because our criteria of syntactic utility only govern the essential form. We lose much in the process, but we have identified what elements and relationships make sense formally.

This exercise demonstrates some of the limitations of logic. Standard logics do not deal well with **propositions**. **Actors** are usually unclearly identified. **Norms** and **conventions** cannot be taken into account fully, so political situations, for example, are missed. **Paradoxes** must be resolved and cannot be retained as elements of a system. Similarly for **ambiguities**. The differences between **logical truth** and **factual truth** must always be maintained and cannot be built into the system as a usable distinction when it might be needed.

The use and limits of logical analysis

There are three concepts which are key to the use of logical analysis: integrity, consistency, and validity. The integrity of a text reflects the intentions of the author. We can test for the integrity of a text by comparing the original text with the formalized version. The formalization should be a demonstrably complete translation. Logical texts also need to be consistent. They must preserve usage of vocabulary throughout the text. For example, the term "students" in the passage above always refers to the same set of people properly enrolled in the institution. Validity is a larger concept because it brings in the notion of what is "correct" within the formalization. So that in a deduction, conclusions are derived from predicates by means of manipulations which have to preserve the referents at each stage. The concept can be applied to induction and other logical forms so that what is valid in one part is valid throughout.

Logic is most commonly studied for its mathematical interest. For this reason there has been a concentration on those types of inference which are common in mathematical reasoning. Logic associated with the common use of language and with the relationships associated with the construction and analysis of information systems is less well developed. Despite this, logic as developed for mathematicians has come to be applied willy nilly to the study of information. Here we will consider just what aspects might be useful to us and where we might expect a more appropriate type of formalism to apply. We will consider two traditional forms of logic and indicate how they may be used.

Propositional logic covers the relationships between sentences. We can express the logic in terms of its vocabulary and the rules that it uses for forming long expressions which have integrity, consistency and validity.

Vocabulary for Propositional Logic:

1) there are an infinite number of possible sentences which can be expressed by variables: p, q, r, s, t, p_1, q_1, . . . p_2, q_2 . . .
2) there are logical connectives: $\sim$, $\&$, $\vee$, $\rightarrow$, $\equiv$ [not, and, or, implies, is equivalent to]
3) parentheses: ( ) to disambiguate terms

Rules for Propositional Logic:

1) Every sentence which is used as a variable is a well-formed formula ["wff"]
2) If α and β are arbitrary wffs, then (a) $\sim \alpha$, (b) $(\alpha \,\&\, \beta)$, (c) $(\alpha \vee \beta)$, (d) $(\alpha \rightarrow \beta)$ and (e) $(\alpha \equiv \beta)$ are also wffs
3) An expression is a wff if and only if it has been constructed by these rules

With propositional logic we can, for example, decide whether a complex statement is always true, and therefore tautological, or contradictory. This is important because we can be certain that operations which are supposed to do more than define things for us are not just referring to themselves. Tautologies are useful when they provide some clarity, but often complex texts hold implications that they are doing more than that. Contradictions are more obviously problematic and using logic to weed them out is usually an important part of formalizing.

With propositional logic we can put together long statements and perform complex deductive inferences. For example, $(\alpha \,\&\, \beta) \equiv x \rightarrow \sim y$ can be a statement with some significance and can be read as "if alpha and beta are equivalent to x, then y cannot be." Or we could imagine it as a phrase such as "if sunshine and warmth is the same as good weather, then we cannot say that it is stormy."

One of the most popular advanced programming languages, PROLOG, is directly based on propositional logic. Its utility in solving large problems is a mark of the power of the careful application of simple principles.

Predicate logic provides the means to analyze the elements of sentences and the operators for manipulating them. This breaks down formality to a level lower than a sentence; here the world is made up of objects and their predicates. Predicate logic also has a vocabulary and a grammar of connectives, as well as a set of syntactic rules to specify well-formed formulas.

Vocabulary for Predicate Logic

1) individual constants   *a, b, c, d* . . .
2) individual variables   *x, y, z* . . .
3) predicate constants   *A, B, C, D* . . .
4) predicate variables   Φ, Ψ, X
5) sentence variables   *p, q, r* . . .
6) quantifiers   ∃, ∀ [there exists, for every]
7) logical connectives   ~, &, V, →, ≡
8) parentheses   ( )

Rules for Predicate Logic

1) Every sentence variable is a well-formed formula
2) If t_1 is an individual term (constant or variable) and *P* is a one-place predicate term, then $P(t_1)$ is a well-formed formula
3) If t_1 and t_2 are individual terms and *P* a two-place predicate term, then $P(t_1, t_2)$ is a well-formed formula
4) If $t_1, t_2 . . . t_n$ are individual terms and *P* is an *n*-place predicate, then $P(t_1, t_2 . . . t_n)$ is a well-formed formula
5) If *x* is an individual variable and α a well-formed formula in which *x* occurs as a free variable, then ∃*x* α is a well-formed formula
6) If *x* is an individual variable and α a well-formed formula in which *x* occurs as a free variable, then ∀*x* α is a well-formed formula
7) If α and β are well-formed formulas, the (i) ~ α, (ii) α & β, (iii) (α V β), (iv) (α → β) and (v) (α V y ≡ β) are well-formed formulas
8) A well-formed formula that does not contain any free variables is a sentence
9) Only the formulas constructed in accordance with these rules are well-formed formulas

With predicate logic we can construct complex formal statements, such as: ∀t_1 ∃*x* (α & β) ≡ $P(t_1, t_2)$ which might be interpreted as "for every t_1 there exists an *x* of α and β, this is equivalent to the predicate term (t_1, t_2)." Or, we could translate it into: "for every boring class there is a group of students who earn bad grades and lodge complaints. This is equivalent to a demoralized student body."

The differences in grammar, vocabulary and rules between propositional logic and predicate logic include not only the greater scope of predicate logic, but also its flexibility.

Nevertheless, in order to deal with the kinds of formality which we need to analyze and design information systems, we need even greater flexibility and power. There are other logics, such as **modal** and **deontic** logics which provide the power to deal with probability, duties and responsibilities. These are the kinds of operators we need when we wish to formalize complex texts, especially for legal and social applications. Modal and deontic logics can be used to accommodate more requirements, bringing us closer to our goal of formalizing useful texts. They deal with possibility and certainty, two concepts which are common in all kinds of business situations, especially where legislation or regulations are involved. Nevertheless, we still need to accommodate time and a logic which reflects the structure of behavior, or action.

At this point we can begin to see how very limited formal logics are, a recognition which should be enough of a caution to us to keep us from launching into complicated formalizations before we have explored its utility for a particular context.

Objectivist versus subjectivist models of reality

Searle's rules for the structure of actions link minds to actions in a way which allows us to take a radically "contextualist" viewpoint. The same connection can be seen to exist between contexts and the kinds of logical forms which are available for our analysis. Given that no one logic can be made to apply to all forms of real life conditions, there cannot be a single form of reality which is formalizable. Before we can take the step of formalizing, we need to be confident of the formalizability of statements.

Our concern with formalizability is related to the concept of the correspondence of a belief, judgment or affirmation and its correspondence to reality. We need to be assured that it captures and portrays how things stand in the world. But it is not just the concept of a formalizable reality which is important, but the use that we make of it. How does the notion of correspondence function in practice?

Our notion of reality performs a number of functions which can be classified in three ways, discriminatory, rhetorical, and materialist functions.

The discriminatory function is the one which allows us to sort out our beliefs into a framework. We can distinguish between those that work and those that do not; those which are appropriate for a limited context and those which we might rely upon under most normal conditions.

The rhetorical function concerns our use of truth as a part of an argument, in criticism, or for persuasion. We want to be able to know whether a particular claim is true, but truth is invoked as something different from any received opinion; it transcends mere belief. When we label something, we invest it with overtones of transcendence and authority.

The materialist approach assumes a common external environment that has a determined structure. The precise degree of stability is not known, but it is stable enough for many practical purposes. The external environment is assumed to be the cause of our experience, and the common referent of our discourse.

In sum, it is easy to accept that people should sort and select beliefs within a notion of reality, and that they should affirm them and support areas of consensus with authority. We can also see how syntactics relates beliefs to causes which are external to individuals.

The greater challenge comes when we investigate the borders between what can be formalized and what is impractical to formalize. How can we tell whether something needs to be formalized, how do we know that it is possible to gain something from the process? The purpose of formalizing is to do something with the formalism, such as checking the systemic character of the whole, or preparing some function for automation.

We could formalize the work rota for the pizzeria by assigning values and making sure no unnecessary tautologies or contradictions exist. It might help us to set up a schedule, but it could not preserve the *ad hoc* character of the business. Since such informality is a feature of all organizations, the loss of spontaneity could be serious.

The traditional distinction between formal domains and informal domains is that formal domains are made up of objects which are readily identified and exist within a regulated, clearly bounded area. Informal domains are made up of things that need to be interpreted and hence are based on experience and subjective, personal identification rather than objective methods used in formal domains.

There is a third category of semi-formal domains which combine formal and informal aspects in one integrated application. In some cases the formal and informal aspects may be separated into different components of the overall system, as with a formal structure with informal activities. Legislation is the easiest example to consider, but this is also the problem at the heart of the construction and application of computer based expert systems.

Finally, there is a close relationship between the problems of organization that require a mechanistic solution and the design of formal information systems. Syntactics allows us to look for general methods and widely encountered structures in the analysis of systems. Our goal is to avoid descriptions which are as complicated as the systems they seek to describe.

Discussion issues

1. Discuss the problems of subjectivism in relation to the standardization of spare part for cars.

2. What are the problems of using natural language for the specification of technical systems?

3. If formal statements can be legitimately translated into several different natural language forms, then is there any advantage in using natural language where formal language might be used?

4. Is it necessary to know the grammar of a language to make yourself understood?

5. Compare formal systems of logic with the logical structure of the U.S. president's State of the Union Address.

6. Consider the semi-formal character of law and find analogous semi-formal domains. Where are the boundaries and what would characterize the syntactic elements of the formal parts?

Exercises

1. By applying propositional logic, translate the following wff into three different possible sentences in English: $(\alpha \rightarrow \beta) \vee \sim x$

2. By applying predicate logic, translate the following statement into symbolic form: "There are computers and telephones which are connected so that one computer is connected to two telephones, but the other computer is only connected to one telephone."

3. Explain why modal and deontic logics are better suited for information systems analysis and design. Comment on their limitations.

4. Formalize the following text:
   "Before any subject is open to debate it is necessary, first, that a motion be made by a member who has obtained the floor; second, that it be seconded (with certain exceptions); and third, that it be stated by the chair,

that is, by the presiding officer. The fact that a motion has been made and seconded does not put it before the assembly, as the chair alone can do that. He must either rule it out of order, or state the question on it so that the assembly may know what is before it for consideration and action, that is, what is the *immediately pending question*."

from: *Robert's Rules of Order*

5. Construct a syntax of your own for checking a book out of the library. Provide a complete vocabulary and some rules for the necessary grammar.

6. Take the following formal statement and translate it into three different natural language forms:
$$\forall S(h) \; \exists G \rightarrow \;>50\%$$

Suggested reading

Allwood, J., Andersson, L.-G., and Dahl, Ö., *Logic in Linguistics*, Cambridge: Cambridge University Press, 1977.
An excellent textbook explaining the use of various logics in the most appropriate way for students of information.

Barnes, Barry, *Interests and the Growth of Knowledge*, London: Routledge and Kegan Paul, 1976.
The most rigorous statement of the relativist position for the sociology of knowledge, as worked out for science as much as for other forms of knowledge.

Kalish, D. and Montigue, R., *Logic; Techniques of Formal Reasoning*, New York: Harcourt, Brace & World, 1964.
A comprehensive logic textbook which is difficult but worthwhile.

6 Empirics

- *Communication theory and information theory*
- *Modulation*
- *Signals and signalling*
- *Codes*
- *Logical measures of information*

Communications engineers will aim to produce channels which assure clear and unambiguous signals, and to exploit the capacity of every channel fully. When a signal is sent out, there must be a code by which it may be interpreted. Various properties of different types of transmission channels have been identified in communications engineering such as noise, distortion, and redundancy. These properties can be measured and permit the engineer to compare and to evaluate the different channels available. Empirics concerns this transmission of signals, and their coding and decoding by interpreters. In this chapter we will explain the role of the physical and engineering aspects of information within the structure of semiotics.

Communication theory and information theory

To understand the relationship between information and the physical and engineering aspects of transmission, we need a theory to explain the behavior of the various components in the communication process. Such a theory will allow us to predict, control, and design information systems where the means of communication matches the requirements of the organization. In other words, the procedures and structures can be designed in concert with the meanings and intentions. The theory that we have introduced in the preceding chapters makes this possible by separating the four different levels of semiotics involved in information and showing how every level performs a particular function while remaining interdependent. This interdependence means that whatever the conditions in which information is used, we must be able to apply empirics to our analysis and design.

When the term "information theory" has been used in the study of information systems, it has generally been associated with those aspects of communication centering on the physical transmission of the signal. Sending messages in the past involved the same sorts of problems as moving any physical object. We might draw the parallel with bygone times when messengers, on foot or on horseback, carried messages from one city to another. Their concern was to deliver letters and the contents as such were of little interest to them. In those days the communications engineer might have concentrated upon improving road and rail services to lead to more efficient signalling.

With modern telecommunications the stress has changed to emphasise those problems concerning capacity, reliability, and relative cost. A highly developed branch of engineering now exists to tackle such problems. By following a semiotic structure to do this kind of work the engineer is able to disregard the meanings of the signals being sent and received, and of the intentions of the senders of those signals, because these have previously been firmly established. The focus of interest is to design efficient communication channels across which the participants in a "conversation" may send and receive signals reliably.

In effecting communication, the "conversers" will employ signals which conform to some syntax, grammar or protocol, and will make use of some transmission mechanism to complete the process. We have resolved the social complexities and can address the technical questions. Notice that the problem of syntactics, covered in Chapter 5, has also been resolved at this level. For everyday communication this would mean that the choice of which language to speak in, for example, has been settled, and the problem remains of how best to deliver the actual signals; that is, by telephone, face-to-face, by letter, or by some third person. If the person who is speaking to us makes some grammatical errors in the use of English, this would present a problem at the level of syntactics. Whereas, if the person fails to speak clearly or loudly enough, then this would be a problem of empirics.

Empirics can subsume communications engineering and incorporate its valuable contribution. But the scope of this contribution has to be restated: it relates to a very narrow part of the whole field of information. By including this contribution, empirics only concerns us after the larger questions have been resolved. Deciding on which means and patterns to employ to deliver a message, important though it may be, pales in comparison with the vexing problem of deciding what to say. By using the semiotic approach we gain something in the process: the measures of information developed by communications engineers may be applied to any type of sign or signal, since semiotics is the study of all sign processes. We do not restrict our interest solely to the common conceptions of signalling: by telephone, telegraph and telecommunications generally. Instead we may employ empirics to any sign that an agent is capable of interpreting.

Modulation

Signalling requires a channel of communication which is capable of being modulated. A flag which is always at half mast cannot be used to signal a doleful event since a change cannot be manifested in that channel. In the same way, wearing a shamrock to celebrate St. Patrick's Day has less significance if the person always wears one.

When signals are transmitted through a telephone system they are modulated. This is a feature of all signal transmission: a signal can be any pattern carried by one medium imposing correlated patterns upon another by a process of modulation. This process entails some input passing through a modulator and resulting in some output signal carried by the modified energy, material, or activity.

With the radio, for example, we can discern a sound wave as an input signal, carried by a radio frequency wave, passing through the modulator of the transmitter circuitry and emerging as output in the form of a transmissible radio signal. Similarly, for a camera the input would be light from objects, the modulator would be the camera and developing process, the carrier would be the film, and the output the photograph.

Noise, distortion, accuracy, speed and redundancy are all characteristics of modulation and each poses particular problems. Occasionally, when tuning in to your favorite radio station, you may find that another signal is being picked up on that frequency, perhaps a conversation between two radio hams. Try as you may, you cannot achieve a clear and uninterrupted reception of your desired program. The interruptions that the conversation causes can be referred to as noise, in the sense that they are extraneous to the signal that you are interested in. By the same token however, to the two persons using their ham radios, your program is noise.

There are a number of characteristics of modulation which are common to all the media which may be used for signalling. Firstly, the input must convey sufficient energy to have an impact on the modulation process. This is referred to as **sensitivity**; the technical capacity of the receiver to discern the energy in the signal emitted by the transmitter. For example, we use the term sensitivity to describe the attributes of a television receiver and aerial. Secondly, the **range** of sensitivity is crucial for the process. The human ear is only sensitive to sound waves in the range 20 to 20,000 cycles per second.

Outside this range there will be distortion or a person will discern no signal at all. Thirdly, the **resolution** of the output signal determines the accuracy of the form of the relayed input signal. The screen on a typical computer system might have a resolution of 640 x 400 pixels. The higher the resolution the greater the precision of any images carried by this system.

In addition, distortion is caused by fluctuations in the smooth functioning of the modulator. So there is always a danger, when relying on word of mouth transmission, that mistakes or extraneous matter will be introduced into the signal. Up to a point we are able to cope with distortion by further processing the signal, and so still make an accurate interpretation. To illustrate distortion we might take the case of a broken television set where the image is squashed into the bottom half of the screen. We are still able to follow the program and make sense of everything, but our visual pleasure has been reduced. The message is successfully being transmitted and received but the signal is imperfect. As the degree of distortion rises the receiver has more and more trouble in deciphering the signal and this may endanger the communication. Television distortions may be caused by a number of factors including variations in electrical current, bad weather or frayed cables, but in a different medium, distortions can be caused by factors associated with the particular technical characteristics of that medium.

Sometimes, where a channel experiences continual problems of distortion, the message itself may be in jeopardy. In such cases a possible remedy may be some kind of auxiliary control channel. Take the case of the "hot line" between the President of the United States and the Kremlin. This device exists despite the battery of diplomatic channels that serve to facilitate the communication of intentions between these two powers. Fear of possibly mistaking the intentions of one another has led to instituting this auxiliary control channel as a channel of last resort when all else fails.

Signals and signalling

What is a signal? Signals are made up of patterns which are transmitted. In the process of transmitting signals, these patterns are changed in a systematic way. For example, when we speak into a telephone the patterns of sound waves from our speech are transferred into patterns of electronic impulses which can be transmitted throughout any electrical network. When the signal reaches a receiver it is transferred back into patterns of sound waves by a diaphragm. The change from sound into electricity is one stage of the modulation. When we use codes we construct recognizable patterns which we can transmit. These patterns can be of any description provided that a source can send them and a receiver can perceive them.

It is useful to categorize different kinds of signals so we can select which are the most useful and analyze the reasons why a particular signal was used in any given context. We may generally distinguish between static and dynamic signals, so that an advertising poster on a wall is static while a moving electronic advertisement is dynamic. Whereas dynamic signals are transient, static ones are durable. Nevertheless, any signal must be carried by a medium.

Different media have different technical characteristics which facilitate their signal transmission capability. Some are capable of taking a large amount of traffic, others offer high signal resolution at the expense of speed or quantity, still others might be valued because of their availability. Let us consider some common media and their signal carrying characteristics. The new forms of high resolution televisions illustrate one characteristic of quality in contrast to the old standard. Similarly, optical fibers can carry a larger quantity of signal traffic than can copper wire. Transmissions which work through sound waves, such as public address systems, operate at a slower rate than those which work through light or electricity. The choices which an engineer might make would depend on the particular context of the medium and the purposes which are most important. Although telephony is now over one hundred years old and does not have the largest signal carrying capacity or the best resolution, it is still an appropriate technology in many cases, simply because it is readily available and easily understood.

What if our pizzeria wants to consider the options, in terms of empirics, for signalling the opening of a new branch? They may wish to choose the medium with the highest resolution, the most rapid form of transmission and the largest capacity. This might appear to favor high resolution television with satellite transmission. But there are many reasons why this might not be the best answer, aside from cost. What would most benefit the pizzeria is a medium which reaches the right people with a clear message and which relies on transmitters and receivers which are readily available. An information system based on word of mouth could provide the most appropriate signalling system for this purpose. Some form of advertising campaign which encourages customers to pass the word on to friends might work very well. This reaches the right people with a clear and simple signal at low cost: almost every customer would know others who would patronize the new branch. In addition, the filters that we commonly use allow us to distinguish potentially important signals such as those we receive through word of mouth, from the mass of television advertising.

For the pizzeria's advertising campaign, people provide the channel for transmitting signals. They may also be interpreters of signals, but in analyzing this example from the point of view of empirics, we are viewing customers simply as relayers of signals. In general, if a channel of communication can be modified in some way, then a signal may be sent.

By using the concept of signalling within the area of empirics we can embrace more than an engineer would generally regard as signalling for the purposes of information systems design and analysis. For example, comparing the signals emitted from a subway station, taking the normal behavior of people leaving the subway as the communication channel, we can perceive abnormal behavior as the output signal from a modulation process. People rushing out of the subway in a panic might be the output signal when the input signal could be the smoke they have seen belching out of ventilators. Furthermore, as long as we can identify the signals in the message traffic, we will be able to turn to the question of measuring and controlling that traffic.

Codes

In the most simple binary communication channel there will be a carrier capable of sending two signals: 0 or 1. This permits the creation of codes which can allow the encoding and decoding of messages at either end of the channel.

In the pizzeria there might be an upstairs room in the restaurant from which the pizza orders are sent to the kitchens. Given four types of pizzas, Four Seasons, Neapolitan, Tomato & Anchovy, and Pepperoni, the codes might read 00, 01, 10, 11, for whenever these pizzas were ordered. Only two signals are required to transmit the order to the kitchen, plus some way of indicating a start and finish of each message. The communications engineer, looking at the efficient use of this channel, might be concerned to enquire whether all pizzas were equally popular, because if these signals did not occur with equal frequency, then maybe the codes could be improved. Should Four Seasons be six times as popular as Pepperoni then it makes sense to assign a shorter code to the more common signal, and if necessary a longer code to the less common: 0, 01, 011, 0111. This arrangement makes better use of the resources, but notice that we had to know in advance the frequency of messages to be sent.

To design the code we have to take into account the process of decoding the encoded signal. A continuous stream of signals needs to be separated into discrete units so that the decoding can be done. This separation could require another signal, which would complicate the process perhaps, or else it could be achieved by the choice of the code itself. In the second coding for the pizza parlour, the signal for each message starts with a 0, and so every time a 0 is encountered in the signal traffic, the receiver knows that a separate message is beginning, that is, another pizza has been ordered. What do you suppose 00101101 might mean? If each 0 represents a separate pizza, then we can split the signal into codes of 0, 01, 011, 01. Decoding it allows us to express the message with the sentence: "Please prepare the following pizzas: one Four Seasons, one Tomato & Anchovy, and two Neapolitans." Notice that in our example the order of codes does not correspond to what is most conveniently stated in English. This is because the coding reflects the sequence of the orders received from the customers. Often we find that encoding is performed as a continuous process, while decoding will sometimes be done in batches.

Channels of communication tend to be expensive to build and operate. Since any carrier will have a finite size, a designer needs to be able to identify the signal traffic of the application and ensure that the channel has the capacity to carry the load. Too large a channel may waste resources, and too small a channel will become overloaded. Similarly, when analysts wish to find out whether a channel has the capacity to handle a new application, they need to be able to estimate the size of the traffic. An efficient coding system will secure the minimum signalling for a given number of messages. In other words, an efficient system for the pizzeria will use the smallest number of elements in each code necessary to transmit the entire set of messages. So that in the first coding proposed, there was no built-in mechanism for separating each pizza ordered, nor was any consideration given to the frequency of demand for particular sorts of pizzas. To make this system work the pizzeria would need to introduce a separate, repeated signal to indicate separate orders, and more signals would be needed to transmit the same orders because frequently ordered pizzas require the same amount of signalling as those rarely ordered.

We might pursue this idea of improving upon the coding system to such a point where it cannot be bettered. If we can find the best possible code given the capacity of the channel, then perhaps we are close to discovering the average amount of information being transmitted at any time. But first we need to discover a way of defining information for this purpose so that we may begin to measure its content in a message.

Logical measures of information

Measuring signal traffic allows us to monitor, control, predict and manage valuable channels. In order to be able to specify the equipment necessary, the analyst has to have a measurement of the signalling requirements. Just as an airline must analyze passenger traffic on a route to be able to decide whether to use the largest available jet or to choose a smaller one, the information systems analyst must analyze signal traffic.

Systems analysts can make use of a number of measuring systems. One way would be simply to count the number of signals coming from a source. Simple counting may be appropriate at the stage of specifying equipment, but this is a fairly crude information measure because it does not account for anything other than quantity. It cannot be an indicator of qualitative properties which might lead to a reduction in traffic.

A more sophisticated measuring technique accounts for the relative frequency of particular messages so that infrequent messages may be regarded as providing more information. A message from your friend revealing to you that the sun is shining today may be relatively uninformative in San Diego, California where the message will be a common one, but highly informative in London, England, where this is a much rarer occurrence.

Measuring information with a probability based on relative frequency (P_R):

1. A source of information emits

a set of messages	a	b	c	d
with relative frequencies	.5	.25	.125	.125
giving probabilities of:	$P_R(a)$	$P_R(b)$	$P_R(c)$	$P_R(d)$

2. An information measurement
    can be derived from P_R

	2^{-1}	2^{-2}	2^{-3}	2^{-3}
using the function	I(a)	I(b)	I(c)	I(d)
$I(x) = -\log_2 P_R(x)$	=1	=2	=3	=3

3. The function defining $I(x)$ was chosen because $I(x\&y) = I(x) + I(y)$ if x and y are independent messages. That is, the chance that S will emit the composite message "bc" is: $P_R(bc) = .25 * .125 = 2^{-5}$, so: $I(bc) = 5$ and: $I(bc) + I(c) = 2 + 3 = 5$

Message "a" occurs three times as often as "d," so when it is sent there is three times as much information in it, using this measure. By using the function for I(x), we can convert the probabilities into numbers to manipulate according to mathematical rules, and calculate, for instance, the information content in a joint message "bc." Communication engineers use this measuring procedure but it is only valid when relative frequencies can be observed.

Measuring relative frequency is based upon probability. At one extreme the probability of the infrequent one of two events occurring might be minuscule, say a one in a million chance. Conversely, the common occurrence has a probability of 999,999 in a million. Measurements of this kind, however, only have value in contexts of statistical stability, where repeated observations over time lend validity to particular valuations.

A more active way of taking into account the amount of traffic which is used is to assign values to the probability that a certain condition will prevail. If the manager of the pizzeria decides to alter the menu to introduce a diet salad containing boiled eggs and tunafish, he will want to measure the effect that this has on the food ordered in the restaurant and the message system that is used. To be able to account for this alteration in the design of the information system, he can apply a measure based on subjective judgement. He may imagine that the salad will be ordered with one out of ten pizzas and assign an appropriate code. Suppose then that he learns of the popular concern about chloresterol in eggs. He will have to reassign the probability of its being ordered in order to know how to adjust the supply of ingredients that the restaurant buys.

Since measurement is only the process of applying a set of rules for determining values, it is the rules that matter. In choosing a measuring system the analyst determines which set of rules is most appropriate. The utility of measuring derives from the appropriateness of that determination and, if it is done well, then the analyst can rely upon measurements to show size, make comparisons, and manipulate mathematically formalizable characteristics of signals. The analyst must always be cautious about making the most appropriate choice and remember that the figures that measurements produce rest solely upon the measuring process.

Let us look at how empirics can be applied to a typical managerial problem such as employee absenteeism. The pattern of absence might form a signal to management which should be investigated. With the manager acting as the receiver, the signals emitted from the workers by their behavior can be analyzed empirically. The pattern is a dynamic signal transmitted by some register of attendance. It is modulated by the process of taking attendance, a procedure which might be subjected to noise in the form of workers who fail to register regularly. Similarly, distortion could affect the signal if a vacation day is not accounted for properly and the register of attendance fails to correspond to the expected number of hours worked in a week. Various characteristics of this signal can be measured. For example, the number of days absent could be counted, but that will be a crude way to discern important trends. A probabilistic measure might show the raw patterns better, but fail to reveal subtle shifts. With a little more effort, a manager might incorporate experience of seasonal factors which affect job satisfaction into a subjective judgement measure. Here, by recognizing the role of an authority, the analyst can apply more sophisticated tools.

Empirics is concerned with signs as signals and codes. When constructing information systems it is important to be able to quantify and measure the use of information. Once we are able to identify who are responsible and what decisions they have to make, then we can use empirics to analyze signalling requirements. Having done that we can begin to specify the technical support which is needed. Empirics, along with syntactics, semantics and pragmatics gives us a variety of tools for building information systems.

Discussion issues

1. Is it possible to communicate without signal transmission?

2. What measures are there for the sender of a signal to gauge whether the message has been accurately transmitted?

3. If losing a vote in Congress is a signal to the President that his policies are unpopular, discuss how we might express the characteristic of sensitivity of the modulation.

4. Consider other ways of signalling unpopularity to the President.

5. Since different animals have different ranges of sensitivity, discuss the differences in energy needed to transmit signals in an optimal way.

6. Discuss the conditions under which you would prefer static versus dynamic signals. Consider the case of visual advertisements directed at drivers.

Exercises

1. Find examples of redundancy in signal transmission in everyday usage. Argue why these may be useful or necessary.

2. Given the coding system introduced for transmitting pizza orders from the restaurant to the kitchen, what changes would be made if the number of orders for anchovy pizzas increases by 50%.

3. Consider the most appropriate channel to use in the following cases: requesting a job reference from your former teacher; warning of a tornado; dispersing a disruptive crowd.

4. Distinguish between the noise and the signal in the following cases. In your answer consider who the senders and receivers are, and what is the channel: a majority vote for mayor and a small demonstration against the mayor outside the townhall; a letter of complaint to a department store and an audit report showing 15% rise in turnover.

5. Describe the modulation process in the following media. Specify the input, output, and the modulation itself: film, drama, singing, essay writing, printing.

6. Explain how people cope with the distortions in the following signals: television, radio, airport public address systems, newspaper sports photographs.

Suggested Reading

Cherry, Colin, *On Human Communication*, Cambridge: MIT Press, 1978.
An authoritative survey of the field of communications bringing together diverse subjects such as logic, language, philosophy and engineering. The theoretical base is from Shannon and Weaver.

Dretske, F., *Knowledge and the Flow of Information*, Oxford: Basil Blackwell, 1981.
Dretske introduces a theory of information derived from the statistical theories of Shannon, but develops to interest those concerned with the relationship between sensory and cognitive processes.

Shannon, C. and Weaver, W., *The Mathematical Theory of Communication*, Urbana: University of Illinois Press, 1949.
This is the classic seminal work on the theory of information approached from the disciplines of mathematics and statistics. It provides an understanding of the tools needed for work at the empirics level.

Part II

Information and Organizations

The next four chapters show how the ideas and analytical tools associated with the semiotic approach can be applied to organizations. By working through a number of simplified case studies, we can exercise our ability to account for the wide variety of issues and problems raised in business and administration.

Whereas in Part I we were concerned with taking apart the whole concept of information, we have a more constructive purpose here. Now we show how, by taking a broad, well connected understanding of information we can see the problems and potentials of information systems in real organizations.

7 Computer systems and information systems

- *Organizational context*
- *Business*
- *Public administration*
- *Professional practice*
- *Information, computer systems, and the informal/formal split*

In this chapter we consider a number of cases which are based on realistic situations and analyze them to show the application of the semiotic method. So far we have touched only lightly on computer systems. Because we have been primarily concerned with the concept of information in general and the meaning that signs carry in the construction of information systems, computers have been relegated to a lesser place. To redress that balance, we now look explicitly at computer systems. Our purpose is to describe in some detail what place computer systems have within information systems and how the semiotic approach helps us to understand information needs, to design complex systems, and to use more effectively the computers that we have.

Organizational context

Chapter 3 showed that the cultural context of communication gives meaning to the signs employed in any system. Before we go into detail about the kinds of situations which arise in business and social affairs, we need to have a clear idea about their context. Therefore, we have constructed these cases about computer use starting from here.

Organizations can be characterized in various ways to provide a basis for comparison. Differences in size, complexity, structure, and dynamism, as much as differences in function, can affect the way we see the role of computer systems. Because large organizations have many people to consider, they tend to formalize to a greater extent than small ones in order to overcome misunderstandings and to standardize procedures. Complex organizations have a larger number of tasks to perform. Modelling, scheduling, and other analytical tasks become more difficult where many people have to be consulted for their opinions when decisions have to be made. Difference in structure, such as that between a centrally organized, hierarchical administration and a decentralized body which distributes power, is another basis for comparison. Similarly, some institutions are dynamic in that their substantive tasks change rapidly. Some businesses change products frequently or are often developing new markets.

What is the best way to come to grips with this variety of issues in such a way that we can demonstrate how systems are developed and used? Case studies are one good way to come to an understanding of organizations: this method allows us to mimic real businesses and social organizations and to analyze those features which will be most important in handling the relationship between computer systems and information systems. We can investigate the character of change over time, the institution's dynamism, and the role of key actors.

Business

Pizzeria

Consider the case of our pizzeria at the time it plans to open a new branch. Using the parameters described above, we might regard it as a small, centralized, and relatively simple business. However, the management is considering a decision which requires much dynamic thinking. When they plan their opening, they require a great deal of information in addition to the general business policies. For example, they need to be certain that there is a viable market for their products in the new area. They must be sure that there is a supply of qualified staff available locally. The location must be considered, taking into account the area, the position on the street, and physical features such as electricity, telephone and plumbing. To conduct the business effectively, they need to know what changes in management practice are involved, such as staff development and the overall trajectory of the business. New logistical problems need to be considered when redesigning administrative practices involved in, for example, keeping accounts and processing bulk orders. New advertising and marketing practices need to be considered. Finally, what might be a good approach to the grand opening ceremony: do they need a special launch party, or to offer reduced "introductory" prices during the first week?

The owners of the Echo Pizzeria will have to decide how to collect and organize this information and how to use what they have discovered. They need to be able to estimate the amount of the information that they are going to use, the speed with which it needs to be collected, the level of accuracy they require, and the form in which it needs to be stored. After a new branch of the pizzeria has been opened, they need to consider the kind of information necessary for running the new business properly.

Let us consider this problem in three stages. In the first we must analyze the kind of information we will be using and how to use it. In the second we have to design some kind of information system. Finally, we will analyze the business and its use of information as a whole using the semiotic framework. To design a system we need first to look at what aspects of the collection of information are best dealt with informally and what needs to be formalized. Within the formal part of the system, it may be that a portion is best handled by some form of automatic system, most likely a computer based one.

The informal part might include that information which the pizzeria has no easy means of formalizing, such as general market information, local customers' tastes, life styles, sensitivities, dining out customs. Do the managers meet regularly to keep in touch about business trends? Are the serving staff encouraged to converse with customers? Such elements will play a part in the successful functioning of the business information system.

In designing the system, these kinds of behavioral patterns can be used directly to benefit the business. The informal means of dealing with information which comes about most easily may not be ideal for the business. To provide the structure which best supports all the kinds of informal communication desired, we need to analyze and to construct. We must choose the boundary between the informal part of the information system and the formal part, and even what we choose to design as opposed to leave alone. There is no natural division, no routine principle which can be applied.

Therefore, to design the formal part of the system the analyst needs to decide how to structure the rest of the information which will be handled by the business. For the pizzeria and similar kinds of business, we might imagine a division between those rules which are derived from statutory bodies, such as health and safety authorities, accountancy standards, and corporate law, and those which come from the business practice.

Firstly, those rules which come from legislation are relatively easy to identify. A professional accountant will structure the books, a health and safety inspector will dictate what sanitary measures must be taken, employment practices will be prescribed in corporate law. Our information system will have to be structured to handle all of the mechanical applications of the rules. It will have to deal with checks on, for example, the maintenance of cleanliness in the kitchen and the routine transmission of information as might be specified in, for example, tax laws.

Secondly, we need to be able to formalize a reasonable amount of the standard or routine business practices so that the intentions of management are carried out. When the business orders supplies, we must be able to apply some form of stock control. When the cooks prepare food it might be convenient to break down the procedures into a number of routine tasks. When handling money, the cashiers need to have some procedures which protect them and the business's income. When scheduling staff, some systematic method of allocating work hours is necessary. Other everyday matters such as locking the doors at night and sharing tips among the staff can also benefit by being routinized.

Some of these matters lend themselves to being supported by a computer based system. Since they are already structured, it is relatively easy to model them in a computer system. Whether it is best to handle these tasks by a machine or to do so manually is an important issue which we will cover in later chapters. Those tasks which might be better handled in this way include those which are repetitious, large scale, or computationally complex. Accounting is highly structured and an obvious choice because it involves a large amount of routine arithmetic. Organizing staff schedules can involve some complex computations, and maintaining mailing lists requires much repetition. Keeping a menu and price list up to date can be effectively done using a word processor, as with other documents that need to be changed frequently.

All of these tasks might be computerized, but managers must always be sensitive to potential business problems of computer based systems. If we find that the accountant prefers to keep most of the business records in a ledger rather than use the computerized accounting system, then we have to take into account his preference. We should also consider looking for similar behavior. For example, when the handwritten method of updating menus and price lists still finds favor as opposed to using a word processor, then perhaps we have discovered a preference which will lead to using the computer less than intended.

Other kinds of problems become apparent when too much has been computerized: the system might be too complex and would have been better left as simple written rules. Some elements might even have been better left informal. If in the pizzeria, staff regularly switch work hours to cover for each other, a computerized work rota would impose rigid rules. The consequences of this might be that Susie finds that she cannot go out on dates at short notice, as she did before. This imposition might have dire consequences. The rate of staff turnover might increase and the business will find difficulty in recruiting. These problems are indicative of systems which are over designed, and point to unforeseen organizational changes induced by the computer system.

Getting a bank loan

In a business such as banking the kind of information system needed will not be the same as in a restaurant. Banks tend to be large, centralized, complex organizations which are dynamic only within a limited range of activities. Although many of the same kinds of problems and possibilities may arise, the priorities will be different. Let us take the example of one major function of banking: making a loan.

Beginning with the same criteria as above, let us look at the information we should have about making loans. For the case of the particular loan arrangement, we may want to know all sorts of things about borrowers. Do they have sufficient income to cover the loan? Is their source of income regular and dependable? Do they have other debts and liabilities? Do they have a record of handling previous debts responsibly? Do we regard them to be a good risk, judging by their character?

A further set of questions could be posed about the security for the loan. If it is a house, can the bank be assured that it is being bought for a fair price? Will it have a resale value sufficient to recover the amount of the loan, if the borrower defaults? Are the legal papers in order so that ownership is unambiguous?

On the side of the bank, we need to know what the policies and practices about granting loans are. We also have to know exactly what our financial capabilities are; is there currently money available for loans? We will want to be sure that the administrative arrangements are established and that records are clear.

Now we can begin to construct an information system which the bank can use to perform the various functions specified above. Let us assess the information requirements for each of the three elements: the interests of the bank, the reliability of the borrower, and the security of the collateral. The traditional practices of banks provide the first guidelines for acquiring and assessing information about loans. Bankers can rely on their experience of previous loans when they assess risks. Alternatively, they might follow a rigid rule based system using forms and standard documents to get much of the information they need. Some of the information they may need might only be available by means of a computer based system. Since the practices for assessing loans will differ from bank to bank and even from branch to branch within the same bank, different combinations of experience, clerical, and computer systems will be used.

Let us suppose that the owners of our neighborhood pizzeria wish to buy a house. They go to the bank where they have their business and personal accounts and ask for a mortgage. The bank sets into motion the whole procedure for assessing housing loans. Since they are known at the bank because of their longstanding business account, the banker can choose to rely on experience for the main part of the risk assessment. The banker knows how much money they make, what fluctuations in income occur, and how regular and dependable they are likely to be in the long term. Similarly, the banker is likely to know the approximate value of the property in the vicinity of the bank and will not be too concerned about the findings of the property valuer. As for the policy of the bank itself, the extent to which the banker will wish to follow instinct might depend on experience. We can see that a large proportion of the critical information, and virtually the entire decision, has been handled by the informal system.

Nevertheless, there will be a great deal of formality left. Some of that formality will be necessary in order to keep proper records, some to provide succinct data to others in the bank or to tax authorities. However, even friendly bankers who know their customers will want to check various records and to formalize declarations and commitments. For example, the borrowers will have to declare other loans so that their overall income and liabilities can be calculated. Someone will have to provide proof that the property is worth the purchase price. Furthermore, the banker might wish to check that this loan fits into the investment portfolio of the bank. These all involve forms, records, balance sheets and bank statements.

Within this formal system, some elements might be best computerized. The final calculation of the maximum mortgage available to these borrowers and the monthly payments will require a relatively complex formula which takes into account all of the elements specified above. It might be made even more complex when tax, insurance, initial expenses and other costs are factored in. It is likely that all this data as well as supporting information about the decision to grant the mortgage is stored on computer. Some of it might even be automatically transmitted to record keeping systems elsewhere.

The boundaries between the informal, clerical, and computer based systems in the case of the bank, as much as in the case of the pizzeria, have to be judged with care. If, as is easily imaginable, too much of the decision making process is vested in the clerical and computer based system, then there are real dangers of the bank missing out on business opportunities. For example, an automatic review of the applicant's income might have indicated that the pizza business is too subject to fluctuations in income to be deemed a good risk. Informally, however, the banker who knows these borrowers would have good reason to trust their ability to manage their personal accounts. The banker might have a good understanding of the seasonal patterns of the local trade which justifies this particular loan.

Too much can be left to the informal system if the bank relies on the experience of older bankers to make decisions. When new mortgage assessors start work they do not have the necessary background to draw on. For them, the formal rules of processing loan requests assure that all the requisite steps are followed. In this way some of the experiences of the older bankers can be transmitted to the new ones.

From this example we can see that the balance between the formal and informal system is crucial. Often when a bank approves a mortgage the informal procedures, although apparently small in relation to the formal aspects, can be far more important. Here the decision to approve the loan was made in large part long before the formal and computerized parts of the procedure were completed.

Public administration
Garbage collecting

A different set of problems appears in public administration. Large scale systems involving routine services might seem simple, but political and bureaucratic problems frequently intervene. Take for example the problem of constructing a rota and a route for municipal garbage collection. Such public bodies tend to be relatively large, departmentalized and static rather than dynamic. The problems they encounter, however, are often complex. On the face of it, garbage collecting should be a very simple task. Indeed, there are packaged programs available for this type of scheduling problem. However, when seen in terms of the information needs and the function that information performs, it is more involved and lends itself to analysis.

First we must ask the question: what is the garbage collection problem? The apparent issue is simply to allocate resources to cover the district on a regular schedule. To provide the analysis we need to know how many garbage trucks are available, how many garbage collectors there are, which hours of the week they work, and what streets need to be serviced. With these parameters, we can model a computer program which will provide rotas and routes.

But connoisseurs of municipal administration and politics will know that the problem is much more complex than that. No computer model working with such parameters can deal with the garbage collection problem in its entirety. That is because other factors must be weighed along with the ones above. Factors which will have to be taken into account include the political sensitivity of certain neighborhoods, labor relations between workers and municipal administration, and special collection services.

Considering garbage collecting from the perspective of a simple scheduling problem, the allocation of resources is relatively straightforward. We might even apply a commercial scheduling program. In that case, all we need to do is to fix parameters such as the pattern of streets, quantity of resources and number of people, and the program will analyze them to prepare a schedule. So far, this problem is a good candidate for computerization.

In any municipal garbage collecting service, however, any system for scheduling is entrenched in a social and political context. There may be occasional events which interfere with the optimal schedule but need to be catered for. For example, the service will need to clean up after festivals, sports events, and rallies. The mayor may demand that his neighborhood get special treatment or that a politically sensitive part of town be favored. Staff rotas might be affected by the home location of members of staff. Rotas might be changed when someone moves, or to match family requirements, as when a worker might need to leave the early shift when a new baby arrives. These factors might, with difficulty, be analyzed in a way similar to the other parameters, but there are many such factors possible and formal systems cannot capture them all at once. Furthermore, they would have to be spelled out in detail, and some things cannot be made explicit for political reasons.

In an organization which is large, departmentalized and static, there is much which can be formalized. The boundary between what is appropriate to formalize and what should be left as informal should depend on the decision makers and their social and political concerns.

School timetabling

Another example of a scheduling problem in public administration is faced by every school. Consider the information needed to make the timetable for a high school languages department. High school departments are small organizations, static, and relatively decentralized. As with the garbage collection problem, however, timetabling is a relatively complex task and we need information about the available resources, the demand for various courses, and the organization of the school year. To analyze the resources we need information about, for example, rooms, books, language laboratory equipment, and teachers. On the demand side, we should be able to assess the number of students likely to choose French in preference to Spanish. We might also have to concern ourselves with outside pressures such as might occur if the school is located within a sizable Hispanic community. The school year will have to be organized according to statutory policies and practices, such as required hours and the number of class sessions.

Some of these factors can be handled as parameters just as those in the case of the garbage collecting service. For example, the school resources, the number of students, and the required hours are easy to take into account. Again, however, we face a set of social and political constraints. If the school is in an Hispanic community, the administrators perhaps should encourage Hispanic students to take French. Business classes could be scheduled to clash with Spanish lessons in the knowledge that the conflict would force many students to take French in order to be able to study business. This kind of consideration can not easily be formalized and, like the mayor's clean neighborhood, may not be officially acknowledged.

Professional practice

Law office

Setting up an information system within a lawyer's office requires a different sort of analysis. The function of the lawyer is to represent clients and this is typically done by comparing the client's case with previous cases of similar nature. Lawyers' practices tend to be small, very decentralized, and not particularly dynamic. However, the level of complexity can be very high. The legal profession is served by some of the most well developed computer based text retrieval systems. These services provide lawyers with access to records of past cases which may then be used as precedents.

Let us consider the broad scope of information used by a lawyer and the part that these text retrieval systems play in the work of a legal office. The lawyer must establish the connection between the client's case and applicable laws as well as with precedents. This requires two basic activities; one is to assess the possible categories the case might fall into, the other is to compare the case with the large number of possibly relevant laws and precedents. Finally, the lawyer must choose a strategy which uses these elements to cast the best possible light on the client.

Legal text retrieval systems, the largest of which is LEXIS, can sort through hundreds of thousands of cases and laws to find those which match the word patterns and search statements given to them by the lawyer. What the meaning of the retrieved text is must be interpreted by the lawyer. That interpretation is taken by the lawyer and compared with the case at hand. Choosing which cases should be cited as precedents, or avoided, is a delicate task for a skilled professional, given the parameters of the decision. For example, different judges will be reputed to hold especially strong views on particular kinds of cases. The type of argument constructed from citable laws and precedents will have to take that into consideration. Similarly, precedents can be examined to find out what could be the most successful type of presentation for that particular case.

The part of this information processing procedure best handled by a computer is the holding and retrieving of data in the massive legal database. It is too cumbersome to be efficiently done by a paper based system. There is no role for an informal system because of the sheer volume of processing. Nevertheless, we must not lose sight of the information system as a whole. There is the relationship between the client and the lawyer, which is governed by rules but does not lend itself to automation. There is the routine and appropriately computerized process of reviewing laws and precedents. There is the process of interpreting and comparing, and finally there is the construction of the argument.

Using careful techniques these complex functions can be analyzed and an acceptable balance can be found. When we are confident that we understand the goals of the system as a whole, we can go on and evaluate the role of possible alterations in this balance. For example, there is a great deal of work underway to provide legal "expert systems" which would guide lawyers through the interpretation of precedents and would shortcut the decision making processes associated with constructing legal arguments. If these are widely used they will radically change the balance between the present computer based system and the rest of the information processing activity which is currently done by expert lawyers.

Medicine
Medical practice is similarly undergoing changes associated with its reliance on computer based systems. Like the legal profession, medicine was one of the first areas to adopt massive data retrieval systems. And as with lawyers, medical practices tend to be small, decentralized, static, but deal with highly complex problems. Medical data retrieval systems are used both to locate texts which might be relevant for background and to help physicians make diagnoses.

We could construct our model of the medical information system similarly to that of the legal profession. There is the necessary relationship between the patient and the physician, the medical practice which is routinely followed, and the possibility of searching through large amounts of data to help analyze the potential medical problem. One further issue which will become increasingly important is the relationship between the physician in a small practice and hospitals. The use of electronic communication to link physicians to hospitals will become increasingly important, both to take advantage of the sources of information available in hospitals and to arrange for patient care.

Using our approach which identifies the character of the broad, informal system in relation to the formal and then the computer based system, we can analyze the role of the computer system within medical practice.

Information, computer systems, and the informal/formal split
Semiotic analysis allows us to take a complex, real-life case and break it down into parts to see which factors can best be handled in a formal system. The boundary between the formal and the informal is one which must be determined by decision makers based on their assessment of which factors can be handled routinely. Some of those routine operations can then be computerized, but there will also be a number of factors which, although formalizable, are best left to being handled informally.

In Chapter 5 we saw how formal differ from informal domains and how a concept of semi-formal domains might be useful. Now we can see a means to express systems where rules form an important part, but not a sufficient proportion of the entirety to justify any claim that formalizing the whole represents the organization and its uses. In almost any business or administrative system there is a mix of things which can usefully be formalized and things which cannot. There is also an intermediate ground of things which might be formalized, but where we run the risk of seriously misplacing our emphasis.

The examples drawn from business, public administration and professional practice illustrate how the use of semiotic analysis can show the relationship between the formal and informal systems. It can also clarify the role of computers within organizations and help to identify where inappropriate boundaries have been drawn, leading to over computerization on the one hand and over reliance on an informal system on the other.

In each of these cases, tools from pragmatics, semantics, syntactics and empirics can be applied. We could, for example, examine the pragmatical characteristics of the law office by analyzing its norms and conducting a speech act analysis of key terms used such as "claims." We might apply semantic analysis to the garbage collection problem and prepare a schema for clarifying the semantic ambiguities of the service. In the case of bank loans, we can use propositional logic from the standpoint of the syntactics of the problem to test for logical consistency. The empirics of the electronic communication link between physicians and hospitals could be measured using the tools described in Chapter 6. In our next two chapters we will analyze more carefully the character of formal and informal systems.

Discussion issues

1. Discuss the pragmatical characteristics of computer based systems in centralized organizations that you know and contrast them with those in decentralized organizations. How would you characterize the computer based information system of your present institution?

2. Discuss the advantages and disadvantages of the case study approach to studying the use of computer based systems. How would you suggest that the disadvantages of that approach could be overcome?

3. "An information system is a computer system." Discuss.

Exercises

1. Take two case studies presented in this chapter and, using a formalistic approach as illustrated in chapter 5, contrast the conditions in them. Discuss how the process of formalizing the cases eases the comparison process.

2. Choose one of the cases and provide an analysis of the semiotic levels at which different aspects of the case come into play.

3. Take these organizations:

   a high school, a police station, a hardware store, an architect's office, a wholesale warehouse, General Motors, the city of Chicago, a local newspaper, a gas station, a theater company, a management consultancy, an insurance company

   and place them on the following continua:

   Size: large, small
   Complexity: complex, simple
   Structure: centralized, decentralized
   Dynamism: dynamic, static

   Discuss the usefulness of this exercise in comparing and contrasting critical factors which may be suitable for formalizing.

Suggested reading

Emery, James C., *Management Information Systems: The critical strategic resource*, Oxford: Oxford University Press, 1987.
Firmly in the MIS school of thought, Emery enthusiastically espouses the glories of information technology.

Hirschheim, R.A., *Office Automation: A social and organizational perspective*, New York: Wiley, 1989.
The author underlines the need for an understanding of the social factors in organizations if good information systems are to be built when introducing new technology.

Penzias, A., *Ideas and Information: Managing in a high-tech world*, New York: Norton, 1989.
This book attempts to demystify the computer and explain the relationship of human beings and the human brain to the new technology. It examines how smart computers are now, are likely to be, and what role they will have in organizations.

8 Formal systems

- *Rules*
- *Rule based systems*
- *Utility*
- *Limitations*

Formal systems consist of behavior which is governed by rules. These rules are representations of the prescriptions which are used to control organizations. Rule based systems are constructed and the process of making them requires acts of conscious creation for a purpose by responsible agents. Formal systems can be analyzed by virtue of the rules which specify them, and we can learn how to construct such systems of rules.

Rules

The character of a formal system is that part of an organization which lends itself to being described by rules. Repetitive activities tend to be formalized and those activities which are guided by regulations or legislation from outside the organization are already formalized.

Repetitive activities are formalized because organizations need them to be done routinely. For this reason organizations need to write the rules so that anyone can perform the task and achieve consistent standards. Often, repetitive tasks seem to require few skills and people become bored doing them. When such tasks are sufficiently important to an organization they can easily be mechanized, sometimes using a computer based system. For example, making a pizza has been broken down into a number of simple steps so that novice cooks can follow the rules and produce pizzas of consistent quality. The timing of the baking of a pizza is even more routine and can be mechanized, and even computerized, so that all the pizzas being cooked can move through the oven at the proper pace.

Regulations can lead to much the same outcome for slightly different reasons. Typically they encourage standards in order to assure conformity with the law. So the annual accounts for our pizzeria follow a variety of guidelines and laws which come from accounting regulations.

Other activities have a pattern to them, but that pattern is not prescribed as are accounting procedures. The pizzeria staff rota, as described in Chapter 3, is a system which might lend itself to rules, but is governed by norms. Rules and norms are different in that rules prescribe and norms govern by convention. Both are made in an active way by people responsible for ordering behavior. Rules are made by rule givers such as legislators, managers, and professional societies like those which regulate accountancy.

Rules make sense only within a defined jurisdiction such as a nation, a business, or a professional body. For rules to be valid, rule givers have to be legitimate and they need to be able to assure compliance by inducement, whether positive or negative. The two concepts of legitimacy and inducement presuppose that powers are vested in these people. Furthermore, rules must be accepted by those to whom they apply.

Within each such jurisdiction there are people who are responsible for drafting rules. The process of drafting involves the application of syntax to expressions which describe desired behavior. These expressions specify actions which lead to the fulfillment of the intentions of the legislators. Rules of this form aim to satisfy conditions of clarity, consistency, and completeness. When these conditions are satisfied, the resulting rules are unambiguous. Individual rules within a body of rules must cohere and the resultant system of rules should be extendable in order to accommodate changed circumstances.

It is possible to identify a characteristic structure of rules. All rules include a **condition** which may consist of numerous elements, and a **consequent**. The conditions are those requirements which have to be fulfilled by the circumstances before the rule can operate. The consequent identifies the logical result.

The basic structure of a rule

If [condition] $\Rightarrow$ then [consequent]

Operators are used within and between structural elements to provide the syntax needed, such as when rules are used to move from the condition to the consequent. These operators can take the form: and; or; not. Within the condition there are terms which the operators operate upon. These are called **operands.** For example, the term "employee" would be an operand in a rule which defines who works for a company.

Rules will generally have "get-out" clauses which allow a responsible person to choose not to apply the rule. This occurs either when the rule has been inadequately specified for the situations which occur, or a discretional element is seen to be vital. For example, a garbage collection system may require residents to put garbage cans out at the kerb side, but discretion can be applied in special cases, such as for disabled people.

Let us analyze a simple rule and see the way related rules hang together. Take for example a rule which we might find applied in our pizzeria which states that: *if an employee is under 21 years old, then he or she can work no more than two late shifts per week.*

A rule like this will be tied to a **definition rule** such as one which states that:

> {1} an employee is one who works for over 20 hours per week for more than 3 months per year.

These rules might also be tied to **status rules** such as:

> {2} an employee (a) is eligible for paid leave after 2 years' service which begins at 3 weeks per year and (b) paid leave accumulates at 2 days for each subsequent year.

The interlinking rules might also include an **action rule**, such as:

> {3} failure to show up for work without prior arrangement and without good reason for three times will result in the forfeit of 1 week's paid leave.

Finally, **structure rules** can tie major elements together, as in:

> {4} if an employee {as per rule 1} forfeits leave {as per rule 3}, then rule 2(b) is suspended for 1 year.

In a complex set of rules or a piece of legislation, we find that these different sorts of rules are required. Definition rules assure consistency of usage throughout the text so that there is no ambiguity. Key terms which are repeated, such as "employee," will be defined for the purposes of that document.

Status rules have an observation in their condition and the consequent leads to a change in legal or social status. After it has been observed that an employee has worked for the pizzeria for two years, the consequent of the rule alters the employee's status so that they become eligible for paid leave.

This new status may trigger other rules which have eligibility in their conditions.

Action rules are the substance of the rule book and when triggered lead to a change in the state of affairs. The usual form of an action rule is that after some observation, some change is specified. In the case of repeated absence from work, for example, the employee will have pay deducted. The rule itself cannot deduct pay but needs the intervention of a person.

The structure rule has the effect of tying together different rules, just as an electronic switching system might activate several outlets at once. Rules do not apply sequentially; the structure rules permit the system to invoke several rules at the same time.

When a bank assesses a mortgage application, it applies rules to routinize and regulate its procedures. A mortgage is a loan made to house purchasers by banks and other financial institutions where the property serves as collateral. The bank is mainly interested in establishing the ability of the applicants to repay the loan and in confirming that the property is as valuable as the loan. The rules which guide the decision might take the following forms. First there will be a definition rule which maintains consistent usage throughout the mortgage application procedure for important repeated terms such as "mortgage holder." Then we can use a status rule setting out who can qualify as a mortgage holder such that only employed people or those who are independently wealthy can apply. An action rule in this case might be: "If the property is 15% more valuable than the loan and if the annual income of the mortgage applicant is at least three times the annual repayment, then the mortgage is approved." The structure rule would specify that if the applicant is not employed, then the status rule concerning those of independent wealth should be applied.

Systems of rules follow syntactical guidelines which, taken together, come close to being clear, consistent and complete. When they are applied in organizations they become the specifications for rule based systems.

Rule based systems

When using rule based systems as a means to construct a model of an organization, it is valuable to categorize such systems in three ways: those which are substantive, those which concern passing messages and keeping records, and those for control.

Let us imagine that all the staff in the pizzeria have all the information they need, and always stick to the rules. Then the rules concerning the making and selling of pizza will be sufficient to specify the entire business. These are the **substantive rules** concerning the prime tasks of the organization. Of course, the staff would not always know everything they need and will have to be supplied with information in the form of messages and records. For example, they need messages about changes in price or in the menu, or records on people who have not paid their bills. This system could be specified by **message rules** governing the flow of paperwork through the business.

Because we cannot always rely on people to do as they are told, there has to be a third type of rule based system for any organization. This is made up of **control rules** for both positive and negative inducements to behave correctly. It will control how people are rewarded with bonuses and promotions, or punished with fines, demotion or loss of job.

Each of these rule based systems can be analyzed in exactly the same way. For the message system there will be a means for dealing with messages about messages: instructions on where to send paperwork. The message system will have a control system of its own, with rewards for people who complete their paperwork on time and accurately, and sanctions for those who do not.

We can apply the concept of relationships among rule based systems to the pizzeria's accounting procedures. The accounting procedures are part of the business's message system because they govern the maintenance of records. On top of this there is a message system for the accounting procedures which reports on the accounts. This is commonly referred to as the auditing procedure. The substantive system for accounting includes the rules for the bookkeeping tasks, the classifying, and the filing. Finally, the control system here includes the rules for rewarding, or possibly suing, the accountant.

These systems are useful in analyzing the various activities of an organization and help us to identify where problems may exist. In every case they would consist of rules drawn up by the organization to the point where we could rely on the informal norms of the staff. Where people are acting correctly anyway, rules are not needed.

We can draw a parallel between the rules which specify how administrations are supposed to behave and the way a computer program specifies how a computer should perform. As we have seen in Chapter 7, the formal parts of administrative systems are the organizational implementation of a body of rules.

Administrations are usually created to implement rules. For example the U.S. Internal Revenue Service exists to implement tax laws. The set of rules by which they operate form a specification for the activities of the administrators; they prescribe what must be done. Tax law specifies a blueprint for the administration of the assessment and collection of taxes. Since tax laws, like all other laws, have been expressed in terms of rules, they lend themselves readily to routinization. So, everyone earning a regular income is liable to a certain level of income tax. The rule is simple and as long as sufficient information about income can be gathered, the rule can be applied routinely.

It is a short step from this sort of routinized data handling to a formal system which can be specified for a computer. To computerize these rules, we need to be able to transform them into sets of instructions for the machine to follow. These rules have to be written according to the same criteria, because if they are not clear, consistent and complete, then the system will not function as intended. The problem of translation remains, because U.S. tax laws are written in a special form of English which, despite being formalistic, still contain too much ambiguity to be implemented directly in a programming language.

On a wider scale, when an administrative body tries to automate a large proportion of its activities, it will need a computer based system which reflects the structure of that organization and one which is capable of changing with it. Introducing a technical system into an administration will affect the way things are done. As a consequence of that, the design of the technical system needs to be sympathetic to the character of the organization. If it is not, then there will be problems of, for example, misuse, overreliance, or waste. These are implementation issues, but they are also conceptual issues about the character of formal systems.

Utility

There are many uses for formalized systems and we can discuss them in two parts: the embodiment of knowledge and the provision of structure in systems. People who use skills in performing complex tasks generally develop set procedures for working. These procedures can form the basis for rules which help guide the novice in performing those tasks. When the intentionality of the task has been embodied in rules the novice will be able to forgo any concern about the meaning and purpose of the actions and concentrate on following rules. Rules embody the knowledge of rule-givers about how to do things. The advantage that the pizzeria has in being able to specify the routine of cooking a pizza is that it can assure not only consistency but also a simple mechanism to guide new or substitute cooks.

We cannot assume that all complex behavior has a shape which is suitable for systematizing. By developing a set of rules which embody aspects of that behavior, we can begin to provide structure which lays the foundation for organization. Rules give shape to systems of behavior and can provide the means to mechanize repetitious activities. Returning to our example of applying for a mortgage, we can see the use of mechanically and repeatedly applied rules. We can formalize the mortgage application rules in the following way: the maximum mortgage shall be two and one half times the first salary plus the value of the second salary, minus other liabilities. Now, we can create a simple sieve to separate applications into categories of yes, no, and borderline, based on the amount requested. This rule will take care of most cases, but for borderline applicants other rules can be made to apply. In this way the mortgage rule embodies knowledge held by the bank about the nature of risk.

Under some conditions this type of procedure can be automated. These conditions include situations where decisions require explicit values which are available for manipulation, and where they are used repeatedly on a large scale and would otherwise be expensive. Without these conditions, formalizing can be wasteful or worse. Nevertheless, the utility of rules is that they set the groundwork for computer systems: rules manipulate symbols.

Limitations

Two of the limitations on formalization are the problem of syntax without semantics and the exclusion of the activity of responsible agents.

When we manipulate symbols we tend to stress syntax at the expense of semantics. The emphasis is upon the operations and not the operands. The operands are merely symbols whose meaning lies outside the formalism. So that when the bank invokes the mortgage decision rule it is functioning purely syntactically, without concern for the nervous applicant whose future happiness is dependent on the outcome.

The key problem is shifted to that of knowing when to apply a formal procedure. At this stage we have to recognize the limitations of formalism and that pragmatical considerations must be applied. If our formal system requires that pizzeria customers pay on receipt, should there ever be exceptions? Take the case where a trusted, regular customer realizes that he has left his wallet at home and offers to pay on the following day. Clearly the proprietor can waive the rules. Now if the formal procedure includes the production of an automatic account and adjustment of the inventory from the moment of purchase, then we have a problem. The proprietor could fake the date of the transaction so that the account shows the next day as the purchase date. But this means that the inventory will be one day out of kilter. Given the amount of difficulty this creates, the proprietor will have to think very carefully about just how trustworthy this customer is. The pragmatical considerations include: how long the customer has been known, how much he regularly spends, and whether he would be inconvenienced or offended if this favor were not extended. The situation would be further complicated if it is not the proprietor who is taking this responsibility, but an employee. When should formal procedures be breached?

Behind any formal system are responsible agents, people holding responsibility which they can never relinquish. However, formalization tends to veil responsibility by making it possible to shift the onus onto a machine. We often hear people blame computers for unfavorable outcomes, just as a policeman will invoke rules to justify writing a speeding ticket. Formalisms cannot take responsibility for anything, they simply embody the values of the formalizer.

Responsibility starts with the system designer and is spread throughout the organization. When a computer based system is developed the person who wrote the program is responsible for it, but once it is accepted by the management of the organization the responsibility passes to them. Rules diminish responsibility because the people applying rules have as their prime concern the letter of the law and tend to disregard intentions. This leads to mechanical behavior where human concerns are suppressed because of the detachment of procedure and substance. You are more interested in how you do things than what you are doing. Your concern is to comply with the procedures set out in the rules and your goal is merely to follow them accurately. In order to construct formal systems which serve the organization most effectively, the analyst should rise above this procedural level and take into account the intentions. The semiotic approach provides guidelines for doing this and a means of expressing these different concerns. It is necessary to encapsulate the intentionality of participants so that the purposes of organizations can be taken into account in the design of systems. Shifting the parameters used in the construction of rule based systems can lead to disaster unless the pragmatic and semantic dimensions have been incorporated.

Rules apply in particular conditions. When those conditions change, then those rules fail. However, principles have general applications. Formalisms are built on rules not principles. As long as we continue to recognize that difference, we will be able to use rules appropriately.

Discussion issues

1. Must bureaucratic work always be boring?

2. Why are some skills made accessible to the novice by rules whereas others are not? For example, compare automobile mechanics with performing magic tricks.

3. Can rule driven behavior ever be intelligent?

Exercises

1. Take a body of rules that you use (such as a club's regulations or the rules for checking out books from the library) and categorize each one into definition, status, action, and structure rules.

2. Draw up guidelines for deciding what should be formalized and what should not be in your classroom.

3. How can responsibility be identified in complex organizations when something happens outside the routine? Consider the case where a bank debits a customer's account by ten times more than the check was written out for.

Suggested reading

Crozier, Michael, *The Bureaucratic Phenomenon*, Chicago: University of Chicago Press, 1964.
An examination of bureaucracies in modern organizations which argues that they can only be understood in terms of their cultural context. This analysis of French public service reveals the role of the patterns of power relationships in the rise of routine behavior.

Gilad, B. and Gilad, T., *The Business Intelligence System, a new tool for competitive advantage*, New York: AMACOM, 1988.
The Gilads present what they call a "formal business intelligence process" as a formal system which can resolve the problems of remaining competitive in business.

9 Informal systems

- *The "real" information system*
- *Social behavior and systems*
- *Jurisdiction*
- *Where the formal system fits in*
- *Methods of studying informal systems*

We have seen in Chapter 7 how real information systems behave, and have investigated in Chapter 8 what characterizes the formal aspects of such systems. It is apparent, however, that no matter how careful we are in analyzing and designing formal aspects of information systems, these parts will only make up a small portion of the total system. For this reason we have to approach information systems taking into account the crucial importance of the informal system.

The "real" information system

The informal character of information systems is expressed in the everyday behavior of any organization. Social behavior is sustained notwithstanding rules. All institutions are built upon informal behavior; this is the glue which binds their structure. It is rule and formality which constitute the explicit parts of the institution's behavior, but they have no meaning without the informal goals, assumptions and expectations which hold together those institutions.

Different institutions have different characters which reflect the prevailing attitudes of the people who work there. For example, we can recognize a "friendly" office by a variety of indicators. We might notice the willingness of people to smile, to help, and to spend extra time putting visitors at ease. Or we might characterize an office as being "efficient" regardless of any measure of output. We could point to a brisk manner, the speed that people are dealt with, or the impressive appearance of a receipt. Now, perhaps in our pizzeria it is company policy to insist that all employees smile and say "Have a nice day!" to every customer. In that case, the apparent "friendliness" is a result of a formal element of the system. Most of the time, however, we can tell whether such happiness is sincere or not because there are all kinds of other clues of sincerity to which we are attuned. Real friendliness or efficiency might be part of a norm for the institution and therefore internalized in the behavior and attitudes of the staff. Then it is unnecessary to require all employees to smile or be brisk in manner; such norms do not need to be explicit.

Norms are the perceived regularities of behavior within a cultural context. It is the way people do things. There are a number of characteristics of norms which have been demonstrated through experiments by social psychologists. These characteristics give us some indication of which elements of large systems of norms are most powerful in common organizations. Using the characteristics of norms described in Chapter 3, we can see the formation of group norms and describe how new members of a group are able to reach agreement more quickly than established members who have vested interests. Group norms are persistent and have been shown to outlast the generation of those who form them. There are many examples of universities with reputations for good parties. This reputation persists from one generation of students to the next without any need for formalities.

Some scholarly social and psychological investigations have shown the importance of group norms on conformity. They explain not only how we can see that people easily conform to norms of dress, but we can see that ways of expressing opinions, and even ways of thinking are inculcated in this informal manner. For example, people reach judgements by recognizing the sensibilities of their immediate group; this is the presumption behind a jury system where only peers sit in judgement. Another key concept concerns the effect of opinion leaders in forming and changing group norms. Opinion leaders who are already established in a group will govern reactions and often prove to be instrumental in changing group attitudes and thoughts. For example, if in the course of establishing the new branch restaurant the most popular senior cook decides to arrive five minutes early in the morning to check the delivery of fresh foods, then it could easily set a norm for the rest of the staff to arrive a little early for their morning duties.

The real information system is the system built on norms and which interacts through interpersonal communication.

Social behavior and systems

Social behavior within organizations is orderly. This means that in any given organizational context we can reasonably expect to be able to predict how social groups will behave. Patterns of behavior in themselves do not determine actions, but organizations have ways of doing things which create systems by bringing together such patterns. Informal systems, where procedures are not rule based, have no fixed definitions of the boundaries of systematic behavior. Observers define the range and domain of the system they observe. For example, within the pizzeria the analyst can discern patterns which define the behavior of staff towards customers. The system made up of these patterns might be described as including their friendly smile, their special attention to children, and their willingness to help people understand the menu. We can identify on the one hand the sincerity of the staff and their friendly disposition. On the other, the informal system of behavior yields to the rules of the formal system, which might include the uttering of "Have a nice day!" and the prompt returning of change. As analysts, however, we must take responsibility for these definitions of pattern and system, and it is up to us to determine just what might be included in our description. Equally, when designing a system, our understanding of where the boundary between the formal and the informal lies is our responsibility, and not something mysteriously "inherent" in the organization.

Systems of behavior can be described in terms of norms. Norms are created by social interaction and include the shared expectations of a well defined group. They are created or modified by a process which involves group interaction. For example, when an office introduces a new computer network, new norms will have to be formed to allow the organization to incorporate the machines. People may change their patterns of communication to make use of electronic mail and so the norm associated with talking at the water cooler may change to one using the computer network to transmit gossip.

A more extreme case will arise when the office moves into a new building. We might apply E.T. Hall's streams of cultural messages to reveal new norms, as we saw in Chapter 3. It is easy to see how new norms relating to territoriality will have to be constructed in the light of a changed physical environment. Such matters as which entrance employees will use to the new building, where people place their cups on the shelf near the coffee machine, or what storage space is used, will all need to be resolved informally. Similarly, new norms will have to be established relating to subsistence; for example, behavior in the lunch room, what conventions of frequency and duration govern going to the rest room, and who runs the errands such as bringing coffee. A third area we might consider is that of interaction. Norms of behavior are needed for office chats, the formation of informal social groupings, and the relationship with other users of the building. Analyzing the informal system requires us to examine normative behavior.

The cultural patterns described in Chapter 3 as perceptive, affective and denotative can be taken, along with our concept of the role of norms in informal systems, to develop a concept of organizational "culture." These cultural patterns are passed on from one generation of employees to another without formal rules, and organizations can take advantage of this process when the informal culture is seen to be advantageous. By contrast, steps can be taken to eliminate negative aspects of an informal system. For example, where an informal social group has come together which is disruptive, space for the reestablishment of more constructive norms can be made by changing the territory: relocating the department.

In a given organization such as our pizzeria, what is acceptable as a "well done" pizza, or as "good" service, is based upon normative behavior which will be transmitted to new employees. These are passed on without having been written up in a rule book. Where norms can be developed without the intervention of elaborate formal rules, institutions can benefit greatly from reducing costs. Such costs include maintaining the formal system, supervision, incentives, and other expensive aspects of bureaucracy.

Viewing the behavior of institutions in terms of norms reveals their systematic character. When coupled with rules, we can begin to analyze the relationship between the formal and informal parts of large and complex systems.

Jurisdiction

The boundaries within which particular interpretations of norms are practiced define their jurisdiction. These boundaries are drawn by members of a particular culture or thought community. In any organization there may be several overlapping jurisdictions leading to conflicts which can cause severe problems for businesses. Conflicts which result from different jurisdictions can, for example, lead to culture shock or even overt confrontations.

Consider the situation where employees who come from a technical background will typically belong to a different thought community from managers. So that a director who asks "How are things going?" may get contradictory answers from a manager and an engineer. The engineer, whose jurisdiction is in operating the computer system, may feel that since the system is working efficiently, everything is "running well." The manager, on the other hand, looking at falling sales figures, has a different opinion. There are conflicting perceptive, evaluative and denotative norms at work. The engineer perceives the business problem in terms of the efficiency of the machine, whereas the manager will be looking at the overall business performance. Their attitudes towards evaluation will rest on their assumptions about what is important: speed of throughput versus profitability. They will speak about their work using different terms, such as "running well" as opposed to "poor sales performance."

In the case of our pizzeria, if there is no rule about the thickness of a pizza, then there is the danger of a conflict between chefs about what the standard thickness will be. Apart from a potential damage to profitability because of the cost of materials, a jurisdictional conflict like this could be confusing to customers who expect a standard product. This could lead to a situation where the proprietor might intervene and establish a formal rule.

"THE BOSS SAYS NO THICKER THAN 1/4" INCH"

The norms expressed in jurisdictions are often apparent, even to outsiders. Conventions of dress in most institutions vary greatly, such that laboratory workers wear white coats, designers in the advertising division wear informal sweaters, and accountants wear conservative blue suits. It is much easier to draw a line around a state on the map than to define the boundary of informal jurisdictions within a large institution. Jurisdiction is an important but illusive concept.

Where the formal system fits in

The formal system is contained within the informal system. Its boundary is decided by those who write the rules. The formal system has no existence except where it has been deliberately created as a part of an informal system. To be effective, its purpose must be clear and it has to be structured in a way which resolves ambiguities and misunderstandings in intentions and meaning in order to facilitate bureaucratic functions.

Rules are intended to shift norms. When rules are applied then the distinction between formal and informal must also be specified. For example, when Prohibition was introduced in the United States after World War I, the mismatch between rules and norms was so extreme that the law failed to affect the prevailing norms, was widely flouted and had to be repealed after only a few years. There is no guarantee that rules will work where there is a potential clash with norms. In order to work, rules need to take account of behavior; prevailing norms need to be examined. However, where the norm is the same as the rule, the rule is unnecessary.

Consider two situations where the norms can be used as the basis for a blueprint for building rule based systems. Where an organization undergoes rapid growth it may wish to specify those aspects of the existing informal system which have been successful. Then that specification can be applied to the whole of the growing organization. Another case might be where a business wishes to set up a subsidiary. For example, when the pizzeria opens a branch restaurant, it will make rules for the branch to follow which it hopes embody the successful norms of the original.

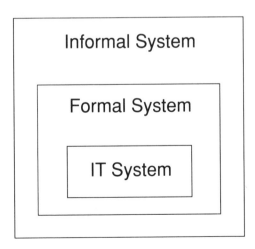

Where information technology fits in

What is the essential relationship between the informal and formal parts of an organization? The informal part is dynamic because people can adjust to meet changing circumstances. People using the informal system have the capacity and flexibility to recognize new conditions which require new interpretations. Informal systems have structures, but those structures are normative and therefore adaptable. Meanings and intentions are used within the informal system in a dynamic way and must be interpreted in order to create formality. The formal system, because it is only structure, must follow and cannot innovate. Rules are changed only when the management wishes to respond to threats and opportunities. Since responding creatively to threats and opportunities is the mark of success, only by paying attention to the informal system can businesses thrive.

Methods of studying informal systems

We have seen that analyzing formal systems is possible by applying the concept of rules and norms. Designing a new formal system similarly relies on specifying a set of rules to constrain the behavior of actors. When it comes to analyzing or specifying an informal system, it is possible to apply a similar concept.

The normative approach can provide us with a technique for modelling norms in a way similar to structuring rules, the only difference is that the jurisdiction is less explicit. The goal is to have the norms modeled in such a way that the specification can fit together to create a blueprint. Then we can use this blueprint to build systems. Like any specification, it can be used to diagnose problems within the informal system. We can use a norm-based specification to pinpoint and alter major characteristics of systems which would not be noticed by using formal analysis.

For example, imagine that the night shift in the pizzeria has a consistently different success rate from the day shift when "specials" are on the menu. The waiters know that pepperoni pizzas sell better at night than at lunchtime, when office workers are self-conscious of the smell on their breath. For the same reason, tuna sells very well at lunchtime. This knowledge could be of great value to the business for purchasing, planning, and other purposes. But this information is vested in the knowledge of the staff and is likely to be opaque to the management. How should the business respond to this when it comes to light? Either the formal system could be altered by resorting to a new set of rules which could be constructed to direct how staff should recommend pepperoni, or the managers might rely on the informal system to adjust the expectations and behavior of the staff by using word of mouth. It may be appropriate to leave issues of this kind to the informal system, where the staff can be relied upon to continue to be sensitive to the behavior of their customers. That reliance and the sensitivity associated with it are inconsistent with formal systems which act by proposing rules and regulating behavior.

Now let us see how more well developed methods can deal with the analysis and design problems associated with informal systems generally. Taking into consideration the context of a business activity will always form the first step in any analysis. We would expect, for example, that any group of people who have worked for an employer for any extended period would have developed a commonality of assumptions which provides a firm basis for the understanding of social actions. Therefore, in this context, as managers, we would not have to concern ourselves with the minutiae of social conventions. Common courtesies can be taken for granted. But distinct social groups within the staff might constitute themselves as further elements which we would have to take into account in our analysis. For example, groups of people who commonly associate with each other can be relied upon to share information provided by the managers. This can act as a means of targeting the dissemination of information without using bureaucratic procedures. By being aware of personal or group conflicts within the staff, and their possible detrimental consequences, the sensitive manager can organize staff rotas accordingly and thereby avoid such conflicts. This should enhance business performance.

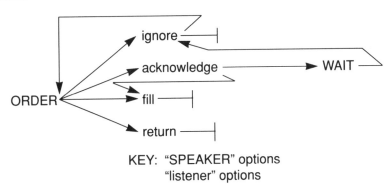

KEY: "SPEAKER" options
"listener" options

Conversation analysis of "orders"

Much of what is achieved in business is accomplished through conversation. Speech act analysis provides one set of techniques which allows us to analyze such pragmatic characteristics. This will bring us a means of understanding detailed characteristics of context, discourse, and intentionality. If there are a limited number of speech acts associated with the core of the business, then it might be reasonable to analyze each of them and even to extend the analysis to the relationships among them. Even without this, the awareness of what stands behind each of the key terms and phrases must be taken into consideration. So that there should be no ambiguity about what constitutes a sincere "order," or when an "enquiry" has been "answered." We might even construct a conversation analysis to represent all possible responses in any of the key communication acts employed in the organization. This is a simple technique to analyze one important aspect of informal systems.

By approaching informal systems with appropriate analytical tools we can specify characteristics of organizations which cannot be satisfactorily represented by formal methods based on classical logic. When we give first place to informal systems in our analysis we are recognizing the primacy of social organization.

Discussion issues

1. Identify cases where the rules of a system lag behind accepted norms. For example, does your college have rules for the dormitory which refer to the sensibilities of the 1950s?

2. In cases where the rules are up-to-date, can you identify what caused the rules to catch up with norms? What mechanisms changed in the institutional structure?

3. To what extent do your local businesses draw up systems of rules to direct their activities? Have they delineated the most appropriate boundaries between their formal and informal systems. In these cases, what are the symptoms of over- or under-formalization?

Exercises

1. Take the case of the pizzeria opening a new branch restaurant as described in chapter 7. Apart from the business rules, a whole area of informal behavior will have to be regularized. Identify the new norms that will have to be created. Illustrate those which govern the use of space, time, responsibility.

2. Where a new building has been brought into use in your institution, new norms have developed. Identify them and contrast them with parallel norms in other buildings.

3. Identify jurisdictions of authority in your institution which overlap. Propose a means of reconciling them.

Suggested reading

Douglas, Mary, *In the Active Voice*, London: RKP, 1982
A collection of essays by a distinguished anthropologist on how society informally creates systems of cultural values.

Holy, L. and Stuchlik, M., *Actions, Norms and Representations*, Cambridge: Cambridge University Press, 1983.
An anthropological study of two domains of social reality: one formed by the notions and ideas people hold, their norms and how they represent them, and the other by the actions they perform. Of interest to students from many different disciplines.

Opie, Peter and Opie, Iona, *The Lore and Language of Schoolchildren*, Oxford: Oxford University Press, 1959.
A fascinating book and a classic study of the behavior of schoolchildren at play. It shows how a large number of practices such as games, rituals, rhymes and chants have survived through the centuries, without any formal mechanism.

10 The primacy of social organization

- *Semiotics for information systems*
- *The value of understanding information*
- *Practical applications*
- *New horizons in the understanding of information*

Semiotics for information systems

Information technology is costing business far more than any measurable, or even remotely likely benefits can justify. Recent studies confirm that billions of dollars are being spent on new computers and associated equipment without any direct connection with business success. Indeed, competitively weak companies tend to do significantly worse after they have installed new computer based information systems and for the most part only businesses among the market leaders are able to improve their standing.

This state of affairs has come about as the result of a misconception of the notion of information. Information has been confused with data and has been treated as some sort of "mystical fluid" that flows through the bureaucratic channels of an organization. This hydrodynamic view frustrates the function of information as the process of communication between agents. A better conception of information makes possible the greater flexibility which most businesses are looking for. It also addresses the effectiveness of business, as opposed to the current obsession with efficiency. Whereas computers are highly efficient in manipulating data, they may positively reduce the effectiveness of a business.

These failures are the direct consequence of a misguided view of the role of information technology and of the methods used to assess the requirements and the context of use of information technology. Typically, businesses approach the problem of implementing information technology from the point of view of the computer technician or, worse still, the computer vendor. What is new on the market which might be plugged into our existing organization? When can we replace the electronic equipment which is overloaded or subject to an unacceptable number of breakdowns? Is it time to upgrade? Shall we use a new storage medium? Are networks and desk top computers really cheap enough now to decentralize the whole system? Can new equipment support more user-friendly software?

Let us consider what these questions presuppose. First of all, they isolate very small issues from any consideration of the information system as a whole. They are phrased in such a way as to assume a technical solution only distantly related to the specific business. They generally allow for a numerical or quantitative type answer and they assume that technical matters are primary. It is that primacy of technology which must be questioned. What we need is not a sympathetic view of the technology which takes the informal parts of the system into consideration, but rather a total reconceptualization of what information systems are about. Only then can we reverse the trend and design systems which deal first and foremost with the use and context of information and not with the technomania which drives so many business data processing or computer service departments.

Technology has an allure which is difficult to resist. The image of technology is associated with efficiency. Having a computer system in your business could be taken as a sign of modernity, but you may have automated outmoded ways of doing business. Often your new computer system will have been designed and installed by people whose conception of information makes them committed to machines irrespective of the information systems in which they operate. The methods of analysis that they will use to design your system will be unable to take account of the responsible agents and will tend to shift control away from effective management of the informal system, which is the key to business success. Such a technical view will tend to lead to a computer based solution whether a computer is needed or not.

We can resist the allure of technology by recognizing that business is carried out using language and that semiotics offers the means to specify what the organization does in a better way.

The value of understanding information

Studying management information systems [MIS] has become a mainstream aspect of business education. In such courses students learn about the newest so-called "methodology" for analyzing information requirements, for designing, implementing and assessing information systems. They range in approach from those which start with techniques for measuring the quantity of data that flow through the system to those which begin by drawing elaborate diagrams purporting to represent formal communication within the organization.

Popular methods include "top-down" and "bottom-up" analyses that attempt to specify the organization as a hierarchy of inter-related processes or activities.

Data-flow diagrams follow naturally from this approach. However, such analyses fail to distinguish successfully the substantive work of the organization from the communications required to achieve success in the business's prime tasks. Even more serious is the mistake of conflating the communication of intentions between the various agents within the business context with the means by which the messages are signalled, processed and stored.

Such approaches, usually only a matrix of assessment techniques, go by many attractive names which imply that they serve whole organizations and take everything imaginable into account. They take for granted that a computer based information system is primary to the organization and that information is more or less synonymous with data. Standard data analyses can then be used to evaluate the efficiency of data flows. Structural changes are often proposed to allow people more easily to conform to the limitations of the machinery.

Sometimes such solutions are helpful to organizations. Sometimes they may even solve more problems than they create. Their place, however, should not be at the center of problem solving activities, but rather as one means of analyzing the specifically computer based component of the intended information system. Assessment and design techniques are useful, but they are techniques, not panaceas.

This whole approach needs to be turned on its head. Businesses should not be primarily concerned with one form of technology or another. They need not be committed to a particular software package for its own sake. Nevertheless, they often act as though what is available is the starting point for building an information system. If a company cannot adjust to the structure dictated by a package or system, it often proposes a reorganization. Sometimes the technology can be used as a tool for reorganization, but in that case its function is an agent of change, not primarily as a means for supporting the information system. When the technology is used as a means of imposing bureaucracy, organizations are liable to increase the least useful aspects of formal bureaucracy although the informal system is cheaper. Furthermore, it seems an outlandishly expensive tool when the implementation of a cheap management consultant's report for a reorganization might work just as well.

Practical applications

Consider the advantages of starting an analysis of the technology requirements from an assessment of the character and meaning of information within the institutional context in which it is used. By seeing the organization's use of information from the perspective of the purposes of that organization, we can come to understand both the organization and its computer needs.

We must start with the context of the information. Most organizations contain a relatively small element of formal activities within a large informal system. That formal part consists of explicit rules and procedures to cover the mainstream aspects of the business. Working hours, pension rights, pay and perhaps laws covering environmental pollution or safe working conditions can all be seen as formal aspects of an organization. Some businesses have gone very far towards trying to formalize their activities: they rely on work uniforms, modes of address, strict group activities, reporting systems which require endless memoranda and confirmations.

However, even in the most extreme of such cases, the informal system is larger and is usually more directly related to the success of the enterprise. What are people's feelings about a company and how does that become a reputation which relates to recruiting the best new employees? Do people care to share their knowledge within the organization? What is the meaning of their normal, off-the-record communication? These factors shape the working environment. Furthermore, for the formal aspects of an organization to work well, they must in large part agree with the underlying purposes of the business as expressed in the informal.

Typically, there is a highly routine element within the formal part of the system. This is what can lend itself to computerization. To work effectively, however, it is necessary for the relationship between the automatic and the formal to be understood clearly. Too often decision makers leap to computerize. Effective systems can only work well as a whole, however, when there is a clear understanding of the relationship between the informal and the formal and where the place of the automatic is understood.

Given the high proportion of expenses associated with transaction costs within modern organizations, it seems reasonable to work to reduce unnecessary control and feedback. But while the pattern is for transaction costs to be highest where formality is greatest, the trend in business is towards greater formality and computerization; a process encouraged by the "methodologies" of systems analysis. This tendency can be reversed. By shifting more activities to the informal, and especially by reducing capital costs and overheads associated with computerization, transaction costs can be reduced. Informal systems require fewer controls. They must, of course, be well structured, deliberate and understood. People in the organization should be aware that, for example, adjacent offices for members of a department can be more effective than the apparent proximity made possible by an electronic mail network. Similarly, by stressing what the organization is supposed to do, rather than how it does it, we can concentrate on the substantive work of the business. Corporate bodies concentrate so hard on how things get done that all their attention shifts to new techniques and consequently to new technologies. But technology should be about how things get done and should not dictate what is being done.

Considering the significance of understanding the context in which information is used, it is important for us to have some guidance, some techniques, on how to analyze the meaning of communications. Such an analysis, alas, does not lend itself easily to algorithms, templates or other formulaic approaches. The key is to teach as deep an understanding as possible. To do this it helps to categorize communication into levels which lend themselves in a more straightforward way to detailed analysis.

Analyzing information from the semiotic perspective is something that managers themselves can do for their own organizations; there is no need to bring in expensive information technology gurus. Indeed, technicians are not necessarily the best people to perform this task, since they tend to have a vested interest in the technology. Similarly, outside purveyors of information technology are unlikely to take the entire organization, formal and informal, into consideration when they do their systems analysis, even if they had the tools to do so.

Adopting this approach means specifying the information requirements without worrying about the computer. Rather, it allows the manager to take the intentions of the business and the meanings of its communication as primary. The function of information is to communicate intentions; it is not a thing in itself. The common metaphor of the "flow" of information through an organization as if it were some kind of mystical fluid, a life-blood, is totally misleading. It is also damaging because, by describing an information system as a plumbing system, the easiest next step is the introduction of a mechanism to improve the circulation of this fluid. That mechanism invariably is a computer system whether appropriate or not.

With a understanding of semiotics, we can investigate problems of information systems which allow us to include all the data and functional analysis into a more sophisticated design.

New horizons in the understanding of information

There is a growing recognition that the way information has been understood in the past has been inadequate. Large amounts of money have been spent constructing systems which may operate correctly but which are ineffective for their real purposes. Often, managers have found it hard to diagnose the cause of such problems. Frequently they have resorted to even more methodical and technical means to reassess and redesign ailing systems. The recognition of this problem is nothing new. What is new is the acceptance of the idea that fundamental rather than technical issues are central.

These fundamental issues have not been entirely identified, and there are conflicting opinions about what they all are and how to go about solving them. Any solution will have to confront the problem of how to envisage the whole of an information system and how to recognize where the key problems reside. There is no technique for doing this. It requires at least some measure of flexible thinking. As practitioners, when you confront real problems, you will be called upon to be imaginative.

In this book we have introduced you to a way of looking at information which incorporates the full range of things that go on in organizations. Advanced texts will give you many tools to use in analyzing, designing and constructing elements of systems. From this starting point you should be able to comprehend not only the way those elements fit in, but also the fundamental ideas upon which they are based.

Discussion issues

1. Why are the payoffs of information technology so small in relation to the amount of money invested in it?

2. Taking on the role of the chief executive, distribute tasks in a business among an engineer, a programmer, and a middle manager for constructing an information system. Discuss what this distribution of tasks does to the balance of responsibilities in the business.

3. Comment on the claim that "business is carried out through the use of language."

Exercises

1. Construct contrasting scenarios where a greater versus a lesser degree of computerization is introduced into an organization. Point out the pros and cons of each degree of reliance on technology. What difference does it make to the balance between the formal and informal parts of the system, and how does it shift responsibilities?

2. Draw a diagram to show the flow of information for the garbage collection problem in public administration using the "mystical fluid" metaphor. How well does the diagram illustrate all the key issues of this problem?

3. What criteria should a business adopt when deciding whether to acquire new information technology? Consider: cost, skills, space, existing investment, the business culture.

Suggested reading

Strassmann, Paul A., *Information Payoff: The transformation of work in an electronic age*, New York: Free Press, 1985.
Strassmann argues that the payoff will not come from the technology itself, but from people. The critical success factor is how we organize, educate and train the mangers of the future.

Zuboff, S., *In the Age of the Smart Machine*, New York: Basic Books, 1988.
This is an easy to read managerial perspective on introducing computer technology into the workplace.

Index